The Six Wives of Henry VIII

A Captivating Guide to Catherine of Aragon, Anne Boleyn, Jane Seymour, Anne of Cleves, Catherine Howard, and Katherine Parr

© **Copyright 2018**

All Rights Reserved. No part of this book may be reproduced in any form without permission in writing from the author. Reviewers may quote brief passages in reviews.

Disclaimer: No part of this publication may be reproduced or transmitted in any form or by any means, mechanical or electronic, including photocopying or recording, or by any information storage and retrieval system, or transmitted by email without permission in writing from the publisher.

While all attempts have been made to verify the information provided in this publication, neither the author nor the publisher assumes any responsibility for errors, omissions or contrary interpretations of the subject matter herein.

This book is for entertainment purposes only. The views expressed are those of the author alone and should not be taken as expert instruction or commands. The reader is responsible for his or her own actions.

Adherence to all applicable laws and regulations, including international, federal, state and local laws governing professional licensing, business practices, advertising and all other aspects of doing business in the US, Canada, UK, or any other jurisdiction is the sole responsibility of the purchaser or reader.

Neither the author nor the publisher assumes any responsibility or liability whatsoever on the behalf of the purchaser or reader of these materials. Any perceived slight of any individual or organization is purely unintentional.

Free Bonus from Captivating History (Available for a Limited time)

Hi History Lovers!

Now you have a chance to join our exclusive history list so you can get your first history ebook for free as well as discounts and a potential to get more history books for free! Simply visit the link below to join.

Captivatinghistory.com/ebook

Also, make sure to follow us on:

Twitter: @Captivhistory

Facebook: Captivating History:@captivatinghistory

Contents

INTRODUCTION 1

CHAPTER 1 – HENRY TUDOR 2

CHAPTER 2 – CATHERINE OF ARAGON 6

CHAPTER 3 – CATHERINE AND ARTHUR'S WEDDING 9

CHAPTER 4 – CATHERINE'S SECOND MARRIAGE 14

CHAPTER 5 – MISTRESS ELIZABETH BLOUNT 18

CHAPTER 6 – MISTRESS MARY BOLEYN 22

CHAPTER 7 – ANNE BOLEYN 26

CHAPTER 8 – THE REFORMATION AND DIVORCE 31

CHAPTER 9 – THE MARRIAGE AND DEATH OF ENGLAND'S PROTESTANT QUEEN 35

CHAPTER 10 – MISTRESS MARY SHELTON 42

CHAPTER 11 – THE WOOING OF JANE SEYMOUR 46

CHAPTER 12 – JANE AND THE PRINCE 50

CHAPTER 13 – TWO YEARS A WIDOWER 54

CHAPTER 14 – ANNE OF CLEVES 58

CHAPTER 15 – ANNULMENT AND LATER YEARS 62

CHAPTER 16 – CATHERINE HOWARD 66

CHAPTER 17 – THE CULPEPER AFFAIR 70

CHAPTER 18 – KATHERINE PARR 74

CHAPTER 19 – MORE THEORIES ON HENRY TUDOR'S FERTILITY 83

CHAPTER 20 – THE ILLEGITIMATE CHILDREN OF HENRY VIII...... 87
- THOMAS STUKLEY 88
- RICHARD EDWARDES 89
- CATHERINE AND HENRY CAREY 90
- JOHN PERROT 92

CHAPTER 21 – THE LEGACY OF HENRY'S SIX WIVES 94

READ MORE CAPTIVATING HISTORY BOOKS 98

REFERENCES 102

Introduction

Henry VIII, King of England and Ireland in the first half of the 16th century, is one of history's most famous monarchs for many reasons. He ruled ruthlessly, was quick to cry "treason!" and execute, and equally quick to fall in and out of love. Henry changed the religious fabric of England forever and left his mark on the wider world – but what of the six women he took as his queens? From the regal and capable Catherine of Aragon to the patient and generous Katherine Parr, Henry's wives represented a range of personalities, goals, beliefs, and influences on the king. Each of Henry's six wives represented a facet of the king himself, whether he liked to admit it or not; unfortunately, a Queen of England at the side of Henry VIII could never be sure of her husband's love – or her safety. These are the stories of three Catherines, two Annes and one Jane.

Chapter 1 – Henry Tudor

King Henry VIII was the second Tudor monarch on the throne of England and Ireland. Born in 1491, Henry inherited the crown from his father in 1509. He was a young, athletic, handsome, and ambitious man with plans for political expansion.

Perhaps Henry VIII assumed he would easily enjoy the sort of marriage his mother and father had. Henry VII was the first Tudor to rule England, Ireland, and France in the 15th century. He claimed his right to the crown after defeating King Richard III's armies in battle, then married Elizabeth of York to tie both sides of the royal Plantagenet line together. In fact, Elizabeth of York had full blood rights to rule England herself, but the concept of an independent queen was not yet accepted at the end of the Middle Ages.

Henry VII pledged himself to Elizabeth of York two full years before his army killed her uncle, Richard III. They were married in 1586, and though they were not particularly well known to one another, the couple is widely believed to have loved each other and been happy in their marriage. In addition to their child, Henry, the king and queen produced three more healthy children who survived infancy: Arthur, Mary, and Margaret.

To the man who would become King Henry VIII, his family must have seemed idyllic. They were rich, powerful, loving, and fruitful – every attribute of importance to a royal family. There was Arthur, the male heir, and Henry the second son, in case the first succumbed to illness or died before having any sons of his own. There were also two royal princesses to marry off to political allies throughout

England and Europe. After his mother's death in 1503, young Henry Tudor saw his father grieve heavily, retreating from court. Every year of the anniversary of Elizabeth's passing, the old king had a Catholic requiem Mass sung, 100 candles lit and the bells of the palace rung.

When Henry VIII came to power in 1509, both his parents and his older brother, Arthur, were dead. In a few short months, the new king decided to marry the woman his father had originally chosen as Arthur's wife: Catherine of Aragon. He wanted to waste no time in creating his own generation of familial happiness, support, and political stability. The couple was married in June after Catherine received a papal annulment for her previous marriage to Henry's brother. It was clear to Henry that his father had greatly desired a connection to Iberia, so he believed this was the best move for himself and for his kingdom.

Sadly, lasting wedded bliss was not something for which King Henry VIII was destined. Time and time again, he found fault in Catherine, then with her various replacements over the years. The obvious reason was that none of the king's wives seemed capable of giving birth to the large family Henry desired. Though Catherine of Aragon gave the king his first daughter, Mary, her continued stillbirths and miscarriages frustrated the king and eventually led him to break the marital contract he had been so sure of as an eighteen-year-old monarch.

In his later years, Henry VIII became obese and chronically ill from ulcers in his legs – but in his youth, he was of decent health and was expected to father many children. The fact that as many as six potentially fertile women could produce no more than three heirs between them suggests that some medical issue plagued the king. Modern medical researchers have hypothesized that Henry VIII may have carried Kell-positive genes, which can cause blood group incompatibility issues and fetal mortality.

If this hypothesis were true, Henry and each of his queens would have had one chance to produce a healthy baby. That one successful pregnancy would leave the queen with an antibody that would attack fetuses during subsequent pregnancies. The queen's body would be unable to support the life of another Kell-positive fetus, resulting only in miscarriages and stillborn children.

If, after one pregnancy by Henry VIII, his wives could only support pregnancies of fetuses without his blood type, the likelihood of a healthy delivery was considerably less. The king's first child to reach adulthood, Catherine of Aragon's daughter Mary Tudor, may then have inherited only Henry's Kell-negative gene, instead of the dominant positive gene. She herself was never able to produce a child.

Whatever the true cause of Henry VIII's lifelong struggle to become father to many sons, it was undoubtedly the most important factor in his ultimate decision to remove Catherine of Aragon from his court and seek a new wife. Unfortunately for Henry and his many wives, each queen in succession struggled to produce not only a healthy boy, but a live child. By the time the king had produced three healthy children, he had segregated them and their mothers to the extent that the happy family unit he'd initially wanted was almost impossible.

It seems that Henry VIII's unaccepting nature toward a potentially infertile woman significantly lowered his chances at a happy and loving marriage. Though the king was certainly virile and capable of love, he was also capable of falling out of it rapidly if babies weren't quick to follow. It's likely that the infamous king's treatment of his very first wife solidified in his character a habit of discarding that which he perceived as an encumbrance - whether it was religious doctrine or an entire person.

In all, King Henry VIII married six times, rarely waiting more than a few days to remarry following the death or divorce of his previous wife. The longest period he spent in genuine mourning was two years, following the death of Jane Seymour.

Chapter 2 – Catherine of Aragon

During a time period in which the nation of Spain had yet to form from the alliances of Castile, Aragon, Valencia, Majorca, and other independent kingdoms, the Iberian Peninsula was a political patchwork. Two of these powerful Roman Catholic kingdoms were Aragon and Castile, famous for their heirs and rulers, Ferdinand and Isabella. Married in 1469, Isabella of Castile and Ferdinand II of Aragon ruled jointly and are credited with starting the process of total Spanish unification. They are also credited with the much more controversial creation of the Spanish Inquisition, in which between 3,000 and 5,000 people were executed for anti-Catholicism over the course of three centuries. Ferdinand and Isabella Trastámara became parents to their youngest surviving child, Catherine, on December 16, 1585.

Isabella and Ferdinand Trastámara were, in many ways, non-traditional monarchs. Not only was Isabella the full Queen of Castile without having to concede to her husband, but she was also considered Ferdinand's political and marital equal. Theirs was a family in which the female children were provided with an excellent education, right alongside the male children. Catherine, therefore, was extremely well-educated and considered very intelligent. She learned how to read and write in Latin, Aragonese, and Castilian, and to speak Greek and French. She was also very well-read in religious philosophy and was taught to hold very firmly to her Catholic faith by her devoted parents.

Princess Catherine's main tutor was Alessandro Geraldini, a dedicated educator who would later accompany his youngest royal charge to England before sailing to the New World. Geraldini taught Catherine math, history, genealogy, law, and a number of other subjects worthy of a future monarch. Her main interests were literature and theology.

The young princess and her five siblings were privy to an incredible wealth of information, not only through their tutors but through life alongside Isabella and Ferdinand of Spain. Catherine's parents, dubbed the Catholic Monarchs by Pope Alexander VI, were not idle royals. They were passionate about the creation of a purely Roman Catholic empire in which no members of other faiths resided. They employed military tactics to ethnically cleanse the Iberian Peninsula of Jews, Moors, Protestants, Atheists, and other people deemed heretics by the strict letters of Catholic law. In watching her mother and father pursue their enemies throughout the Old and New World, Catherine learned a great deal of administrative war-time skills.

Catherine and her siblings were heirs in line to the most powerful regime in Europe at the end of the 15th century. Her options in terms of a husband were not taken lightly by her parents or their respective kingdoms. A number of marriage partners for Catherine were considered before her parents decided on a match with Arthur Tudor. England was not Spain's first choice for an ally, but after having married their first four children to monarchs in Portugal and Austria, it was a timely decision on the part of Isabella and Ferdinand.

This was an extremely strategic partnership on the part of England's Henry VII because there were still factions throughout Europe who believed his conquest of England and Ireland was invalid due to his debatably illegitimate birth. Since Catherine of Aragon was also descended from King Edward III of England, just as were the Tudor heirs, Henry VII thought it best to consolidate that power into one marriage. Catherine was promised to Arthur Tudor before she was even four years old; she arrived in England with the promise of a 200,000-crown dowry.

Chapter 3 – Catherine and Arthur's Wedding

Catherine of Aragon and Arthur Tudor were married by proxy on May 14, 1499. Since they were still both underage, the couple remained apart until Catherine was 16 and Arthur was 15. Over the course of the next two years, they kept in touch via letters written in their common language of Latin. Those letters portray an impatient young prince and a very polite and elegant young princess, both eager to move forward with their lives and stop waiting for the future to arrive:

"I have read the most sweet letters of your highness most lately given to me, from which I have easily perceived your most entire love to me. Truly those your letters, traced by your own hand, have so delighted me, and have rendered me so cheerful and jocund, that I fancied I beheld your highness and conversed with and embraced my dearest wife. I cannot tell you what an earnest desire I feel to see your highness, and how vexatious to me is this procrastination about your coming."

In 1501, Ferdinand and Isabella promised Henry VII that Catherine would soon arrive in England. Throughout the first part of the year, weather delayed her departure several times. In May of the same year, the princess fell ill for a time before finally beginning her journey to the sea at the north of her country. This journey alone was quite arduous, as it stretched more than 500 miles from Grenada to

Galicia. Crossing the country took nearly three months, after which Catherine finally boarded a ship to England on August 17. Even then, the journey was difficult – storms in the Bay of Biscay caused damage and forced the ship and its accompanying fleet to retreat to Spain soon after departure. On the 24th of September, the same fleet set sail a final time under the leadership of one of England's best sailors, Stephen Butt.

Once the refitted ships set out a second time, the voyage took less than six days. Catherine and her retinue arrived at Plymouth on the 2nd of October 1501. They were received by local nobles and directed to their prepared lodgings at Exeter, where King Henry sent a party to escort them to Lambeth Palace in London. The princess arrived in London on the 9th of November 1501, more than five months after her journey had begun from the south of Spain.

Catherine of Aragon had a pale complexion, blue eyes, and light auburn hair; she was considered a beautiful young lady by many who saw her. Said lawyer and philosopher Thomas More:

"Ah, but the lady! Take my word for it, she thrilled the hearts of everyone: she possesses all those qualities that make for beauty in a very charming girl. Everywhere she receives the highest of praises; but even that is inadequate."

The Spanish princess married Arthur Tudor on November 14, 1501, never having laid eyes on him before. The bride wore a thick veil during the ceremony, so she and Arthur only really saw each other after they had personally exchanged their marital vows at St. Paul's Cathedral. Catherine's future husband, Henry Tudor, escorted her down the aisle to meet her brother. Afterward, the couple was publicly shown to their bed.

Arthur's grandmother, Lady Margaret Beaufort, prepared the marriage bed for her grandson and his new wife. She sprinkled the bed with holy water before Catherine's ladies-in-waiting helped dress the new Princess of Wales in her night dress and left her in the bed when the Prince entered the room in his own nightgown. The marriage bed was blessed by the Bishop of London, then the newlyweds were finally left alone.

The morning after the wedding, Arthur boasted jocularly that he'd consummated his marriage with Catherine, which was of course expected of him by his parents and in-laws. Whether he was merely acting the part, however, or excitedly telling the truth, would become a hotly-debated point in history. After the wedding, Catherine and Arthur both moved to the Welsh border at Ludlow Castle to govern their piece of the kingdom. The couple both fell very ill in March, and though Catherine recovered, Arthur died only four months after the wedding. The princess insisted that she and Arthur had not consummated the marriage before her young husband's death.

It isn't clear just what illness the royal couple suffered from, though possibilities include the mysterious English sweating sickness or tuberculosis. Catherine took several months to recover from the illness, after which royal doctors sent by the king determined she was not pregnant and therefore not carrying a royal heir. Arthur's funeral was held on the 23rd of April, and his widow did not attend. Traditional forbade her appearance, though even if she'd wanted to see her husband buried, Catherine was still very sick.

The teenage widow was kept in England following the death of Arthur. Her fate was yet to be decided by Spanish ambassador Doctor de Puebla and Henry VII of England. Henry VII wanted to keep Catherine in the family and he certainly wanted to collect the second half of her dowry – the only logical solution was to remarry her to young Henry Tudor. Fortunately, Isabella and Ferdinand agreed, but the negotiations took over a year to reach completion. In June of 1503, Henry Tudor became formally engaged to his brother's widow. The couple was given permission for their arrangement by Pope Julius II the next year, on the basis of Catherine's statement that the former marriage had not been consummated. So, Catherine waited in earnest for the king's youngest son to come of age.

The years she spent in waiting were not particularly pleasant for the young Princess of Wales, as she was without an income and totally reliant on her father and King Henry – her mother Isabella having died in 1504. In a letter to Ferdinand II in 1505, Catherine was forced to ask for money to pay her lady in waiting:

"Most high and most puissant lord,

It is known to your highness how donna Maria de Salazar was lady to the queen my lady, who is in blessed glory, and how her highness sent her to come with me; and in addition to the service which she did to her highness, she has served me well, and in all this has done as a worthy woman. Wherefore I supplicate your highness that, as well on account of the one service as the other, you would command her to be paid, since I have nothing wherewith to pay her...

From Durham, the eighth of September.

The humble servant of your highness,

who kisses your hands,

The Princess of Wales."

Catherine also wrote to her father asking very politely for dowries to be provided for all the ladies he had sent with her to England. She was very aware of the fact that none of her ladies had been paid to follow her or provide their services and wanted them to find good marriages instead of continuing on in the same manner, unable to buy themselves clothing or necessities. Another letter from Catherine to her father in 1505 shows just how uncomfortable the princess had become away from Spain:

"Most high and most puissant lord,

Hitherto I have not wished to let your highness know the affairs here, that I might not give you annoyance, and also thinking that they would improve; but it appears that the contrary is the case, and that each day my troubles increase; and all this on account of the doctor de Puebla, to whom it has not sufficed that from the beginning he transacted a thousand falsities against the service of your highness, but now he has given me new trouble...

Your highness shall know, as I have often written to you, that since I came into England I have not had a single maravedi [type of Spanish coin] except a certain sum which was given me for food, and this such a sum that it did not suffice without my having many debts in London; and that which troubles me more is to see my servants and maidens so at a loss, and that they have not wherewith to get clothes; and this I believe is all done by hand of the doctor, who, notwithstanding your highness has written, sending him word that he should have money from the king of England...

...A few days ago donna Elvira de Manuel asked my leave to go to Flanders to get cured of a complaint which has come into her eyes...I begged the king of England, my lord, that until our donna Elvira should return his highness would command that I should have, as a companion, and old English lady, or that he would take me to his court. [The doctor] negotiated that the king should dismiss all my household, and take away my chamber and send to place it in a house of his own, so that I should not be in any way mistress of it.

Your highness will see what would serve you best, and with this I shall be most content.

The humble servant of your highness,

who kisses your hands,

The Princess of Wales."

For his part, Ferdinand II deferred almost entirely to King Henry VII to provide his daughter with what he saw as proper. In 1507, after repeated entreaties by Catherine, The King of Aragon appointed her his ambassador in England. With a job and some income, the princess' status and confidence were much improved, and she took her role very seriously.

Chapter 4 – Catherine's Second Marriage

Early in 1509, King Henry VII died of tuberculosis, leaving his son Henry VIII to succeed him as King of England and Ireland. Impatient to begin his reign, the new king arranged to marry Catherine of Aragon just a few months after the death of his father. The two of them were married privately at Greenwich Palace on June 11, 1509. Catherine was 23 years old and Henry VIII was just shy of his eighteenth birthday.

The couple was crowned in a joint ceremony just weeks after the wedding, with much fanfare and celebration. The new king participated in the celebratory jousting competitions and performed with gusto. According to contemporary accounts, he seemed to all assembled the perfect specimen of a king:

"The King tilted against many, stoutly and valorously. According to their own observation and the report of others, King Henry was not only very expert in arms and of great valour, and most eminent for his personal endowments, but so gifted and adorned with mental accomplishments, that they believed him to have few equals in the world. He spoke English, French, and Latin, understood Italian well, played on almost every instrument, sang and composed fairly, was prudent, sage, and free from every vice, and so good and affectionate a friend to the Signory, that no ultramontane sovereign ever surpassed him in that respect."

Catherine was also enamored of her new husband, and the new Queen of England became pregnant soon after her second wedding. In January of 1504, however, the baby girl she delivered was stillborn. It was a huge disappointment for Catherine, Henry, and their kingdom, who awaited the birth of a male Tudor heir. Nevertheless, miscarriages and pregnancy complications were a thing of normalcy in Tudor England, so the royal couple simply hoped for better results next time.

Catherine of Aragon is estimated to have had six to 10 pregnancies throughout her marriage to King Henry VIII, only two of which resulted in a live baby. The first was a boy named Henry; the second a daughter called Mary. Baby Henry died at two months of age, but Mary lived to adulthood and would be the future Queen of England, the first female to independently hold that position.

Despite the royal couple's troublesome fertility, Catherine and Henry were a loving and powerful couple. The king trusted his wife's judgment and spoke with her regularly about the business of running the country. In turn, Catherine confided in her father, and so the three monarchs became very closely-allied. Ferdinand II and his daughter were primarily concerned about the fate of Spain in ongoing wars with France, and in time Henry VIII decided to put his own armies on the continent to side with Spain. Furthermore, Henry VIII was determined to win back France for himself, as Henry V had done a century before. The timing was ideal for such a campaign.

While Henry headed to France to command his army, Queen Catherine became Regent of England at home. She would not be idle, for while her husband was away, King James IV of Scotland seized the moment and attacked England. A Scottish army of 80,000 crossed the English border on August 22, 1513. As a long-term ally of France, Scotland's monarch felt it was his duty to attack his southern neighbor in its weakened position. Catherine, however, summoned 40,000 reserve troops and enacted an impactful victory over the enemy at the Battle of Flodden in September. Not only was the Scottish army heavily weakened, but King James IV of Scotland himself had been killed.

Catherine proudly wrote to her husband in France to send him the news:

"Sir,

My lord Havard sent me a letter open to your grace within one of mine, by the which ye shall see at length the great victory that our Lord hath sent your subjects in your absence: and for this cause it is no need herein to trouble your grace with long writing; but to my thinking this battle hath been to your grace and all your realm the greatest honour that could be, and more than should you win all the crown of France: thanked be God of it, and I am sure your grace forgetteth not to do this, which shall be cause to send you many more such great victories, as I trust he shall do…

My husband, for hastiness with Rogecrosse, I could not send your grace the piece of the king of Scots' coat, which John Glyn now bringeth; in this your grace shall see, how I can keep my promise: sending you for your banners a king's coat…

Your humble wife and true servant

Katarine."

Catherine of Aragon proved herself a true disciple and daughter of Isabella and Ferdinand of Spain, who had managed armies side-by-side during her youth. Unfortunately, however, the queen had been pregnant during the military campaign and worried that the overwork required of her would harm the baby. Indeed, the next month, Catherine delivered a baby boy who died very soon after his birth.

King Henry VIII returned to England soon afterward, having been successful in taking Tournai from France. Ironically, at the death of King James IV, Henry's sister Margaret became Regent of Scotland. Except for the death of the newborn Prince of England, it was a time of pride and celebration at the Tudor court.

On February 18, 1516, Queen Catherine delivered a healthy baby girl named Mary. She wanted to provide the same opportunities to Mary that her own parents had given her, which meant a more comprehensive education than girls at that time received in England. Catherine began to visit educational facilities such as Oxford University and donate generously. Her belief that girls should be well-educated caught on throughout England and became the subject of literature and debate.

While Catherine devoted her time to Mary, Henry VIII took up with several mistresses. One of these, Elizabeth Blount, delivered a healthy baby boy in 1519. Though the boy was illegitimate, there was still talk that he could become the next King of England if his father chose to recognize him officially. Excited at the prospect of a healthy son, Henry VIII did indeed acknowledge that young Henry was his progeny and made sure that he was well-cared for. In fact, it was the king himself who named the boy Henry Fitzroy, literally "Henry Son of the King." Catherine was deeply hurt and embarrassed at the news. By 1519 she was 34 years old and not expected to produce any more royal children.

King Henry VIII began to pull away from Queen Catherine after the birth of Henry Fitzroy, and, embarrassed, she did little to fight for his attention. By 1525, the king had not only begun an affair with his wife's lady-in-waiting, Anne Boleyn, but he had fallen desperately in love with her. Anne, for her part, told the king that she would not engage in sexual intercourse with him unless they were to be married. Frustrated, Henry continued to send the young woman love letters and expensive gifts.

Catherine began dining alone, much to her personal regret, as Henry no longer joined her and their nine-year-old daughter Princess Mary had been sent to Ludlow Palace to establish her own court.

Chapter 5 – Mistress Elizabeth Blount

Known at court as Bessie Blount, Elizabeth was born to John Blount and Catherine Pershall in about the year 1500. As a young girl, she came to court as a lady-in-waiting to Queen Catherine of Aragon. Seven or eight years the king's junior, Bessie caught the eye of her sovereign and they embarked on a relationship that would be quite substantial – at least five years in length.

The young girl was pretty, engaging, and fifteen years younger than Queen Catherine. Blonde and blue-eyed, she enjoyed dancing, singing, and riding horses, a hobby she shared with the young king. Though Henry was still apparently satisfied with his marriage, at least in the theoretical and political sense, he had no problem seeking out the company of other women. In fact, seeking out lovers from among those who served his queen would become a lifelong habit.

The affair was quite hushed, especially compared to Henry's later amorous trysts, and it is possible that the queen was unaware of it. Until, of course, the king's mistress became pregnant. Bessie discovered she was pregnant early in 1519 and was sent away from the royal palace to give birth in June. The baby was Henry Fitzroy.

For his part, Henry VIII was gentle concerning the birth and the unwed mother. He made sure that Bessie and the boy were safe and comfortable and went so far as to officially acknowledge his fatherhood of little Henry, giving him the title of Lord of Richmond.

The love affair, however, had come to a necessary end since Bessie could no longer serve at court with an infant. King Henry set up an annual 200-pound income and property for Bessie Blount and set her up to marry Gilbert Tailboys, another aristocrat whose livelihood now depended on the goodness of the crown.

Before the marriage to Tailboys, however, Bessie gave birth to her second child, a girl named Elizabeth. Though Elizabeth would take Gilbert Tailboys' name after 1522, it seems very likely this child was also fathered by the King of England. Given Henry Tudor's indifference to female children, however, he never acknowledged Elizabeth publicly nor did he attempt to groom her for the throne.

It may seem cold-hearted of Henry not to have kept his mistress and children near, but the king did care enough to give Bessie, young Henry and Elizabeth a life no other unwed mother or illegitimate children could hope for at that time. She had a husband, an income and a place to live in safety with her little boy and girl. Bessie and Gilbert moved to Lincolnshire and had two more children, but Gilbert died in 1530. At that time, Fitzroy was becoming seriously ill and King Henry was personally focused on Anne Boleyn. Knowing it was futile to hope the king might marry her and legitimize their children, Bessie married Edward Fiennes de Clinton, twelve years her junior. They had another three children, making the king's former mistress a mother of seven.

King Henry made a point of becoming acquainted with his illegitimate son, which meant that he did continue to see his former lover for years following their prompt breakup. He brought gifts for the boy and bestowed more money on Bessie whenever he saw fit. The young Henry wrote to his royal father often, thanking him for the gifts and always asking for his blessings. The two kept in close contact, not through any manipulations of the mother but from the pure desire of Henry Tudor to know his boy and ensure he grew up well.

In addition to frivolous gifts, the king provided his child with professional tutors so that young Henry could learn to read and write in English, Latin, and French. The tutor chosen personally by King Henry was John Palsgrave, an Englishman who had been educated in London and Paris. In addition to a dedicated teacher, the boy was also appointed his own council – also handpicked by the king himself – as if Henry were being groomed to become the king's official heir.

King Henry was not content to pin all his hopes of the royal succession either on Mary or his illegitimate son, so he remarried in 1533 despite already having produced a potential male heir. Fitzroy struggled with poor health for several years but seemed strong enough to continue fighting the disease and rallying to health. In July of 1536, however, that fight ended and the king's only son died. It seems most likely that he died from tuberculosis, but some have theorized that the boy contracted a strain of the plague. He was interred at the Thetford Priory in Norfolk but following the Reformation his tomb found a permanent home at St. Michael's Church in Suffolk.

During the short tenure of Anne of Cleves as King Henry's wife, Bessie returned to the English court to serve the new queen. Her service was as brief as Anne's, unfortunately, because she no longer enjoyed good health. Only three years after the death of her firstborn, Elizabeth Blount died shortly after giving birth to her seventh child, Margaret Clinton. She was estimated to have been 42 years old and had lived to a very good age for the time. Much of the luxury and comfort she enjoyed throughout her life were due to her close and enduring friendship with King Henry VIII.

After having lived such a life, it is strange to find that there is no clear information about Bessie's funeral or her burial place. Most historians agree that these details have been lost to the centuries. However, St. Mary and All Saints Churchyard in South Kyme, Lincolnshire, claims to host the remains of one of King Henry VIII's most favored women, Elizabeth Blount Clinton, deceased on the 15th of June 1541.

Chapter 6 – Mistress Mary Boleyn

After the departure from court of Henry's long-time mistress Bessie Blount, the king began to take particular notice of the most attractive girls around him at court. The one he most favored was none other than the sister of his future Protestant Queen, Anne Boleyn. Mary, perhaps a year or two older than Anne, appeared first among the ladies of Queen Catherine of Aragon. Born in 1501, she was 10 years younger than Henry. Upon meeting, she was likely 19 years of age.

Mary Boleyn had had an excellent education that included history, languages, reading, writing, arithmetic, music, sewing and embroidery, dancing, singing, card games, hunting, riding, and falconry. Her first position was as lady-in-waiting to Mary Tudor, the king's sister, in Paris. Though the Tudor sister returned to England as soon as her husband, the French king, died, Mary was allowed to stay on at the French court. She may even have had an affair with the new king himself, Francis I, a rumor that the monarch wasn't bothered to negate.

Mary returned to the English court in 1519, the same year that Elizabeth Blount delivered Henry Fitzroy. She was a grown woman but still young, pretty, and remarkably interesting given her extensive education and time spent in France. The English king charmed his way into Mary's heart but was wary of becoming stuck with another unwed mother as a result of an affair. Perhaps for this reason, Henry pushed Mary Boleyn to marry one of his council members, William Carey. The marriage went through in early 1520 and Carey enjoyed several gifts of land and money from the king thereafter.

There are so few concrete details surrounding the life of Mary Boleyn that it is easy to overlook her, but historians all agree she did have an explicit affair with King Henry VIII at some point during the early 1520s. Whether this was before the wedding, after the wedding or both, is simply unknown. What researchers do know, however, is that theirs was not a long-lived affair, though the paternity of Mary's children – ostensibly named Catherine and Henry – has always been in question.

William Carey died of the English sweating sickness in 1528, leaving Mary free to remarry William Stafford in 1534. That marriage was not sanctioned by the king, a fact that Henry took very seriously. He angrily cut her off from her annual salary and banished her from court. Nevertheless, Mary believed in her second marriage, which was purely for love. The couple had debts and only a small income, however, so the former lover of the king wrote to Henry's most favored advisor, Thomas Cromwell, and beseeched him to speak on her behalf to Henry so that she would not end up destitute.

This letter is the weightiest piece of evidence Mary Boleyn left behind of her life:

"Master Secretary,

After my poor recommendations, which is smally to be regarded of me, that am a poor banished creature, this shall be to desire you to be good to my poor husband and to me. I am sure it is not unknown to you the high displeasure that both he and I have, both of the king's highness and the queen's grace, by reason of our marriage without their knowledge, wherein we both do yield ourselves faulty, and do acknowledge that we did not well to be so hasty nor so bold, without their knowledge. But one thing, good master secretary, consider, that he was young, and love overcame reason; and for my part I saw so much honesty in him, that I loved him as well as he did me, and was in bondage, and glad I was to be at liberty: so that, for my part, I saw that all the world did set so little by me, and he so much, that I thought I could take no better way but to take him and to forsake all other ways, and live a poor, honest life with him. And so I do put no doubts but we should, if we might once be so happy to recover the king's gracious favour and the queen's. For well I might have had a greater man of birth and a higher, but I assure you I could never have had one that should have loved me so well, nor a more honest man; and besides that, he is both come of an ancient stock, and again as meet (if it was his grace's pleasure) to do the king service, as any young gentleman in his court.

Therefore, good master secretary, this shall be my suit to you, that, for the love that well I know you do bear to all my blood, though, for my part, I have not deserved it but smally, by reason of my vile conditions, as to put my husband to the king's grace that he may do his duty as all other gentlemen do. And, good master secretary, sue for us to the king's highness, and beseech his highness, which ever was wont to take pity, to have pity on us; and that it will please his grace of his goodness to speak to the queen's grace for us; for, so far as I can perceive, her grace is so highly displeased with us both that, without the king be so good lord to us as to withdraw his rigour and sue for us, we are never like to recover her grace's favour: which is too heavy to bear. And seeing there is no remedy, for God's sake help us; for we have been now a quarter of a year married, I thank God, and too late now to call that again; wherefore it is the more almones [alms] to help. But if I were at my liberty and might choose, I ensure you, master secretary, for my little time, I have tried so much honesty to be in him, that I had rather beg my bread with him than to be the greatest queen in Christendom. And I believe verily he is in the same case with me; for I believe verily he would not forsake me to be a king.

Therefore, good master secretary, seeing we are so well together and does intend to live so honest a life, though it be but poor, show part of your goodness to us as well as you do to all the world besides; for I promise you, you have the name to help all them that hath need, and amongst all your suitors I dare be bold to say that you have no matter more to be pitied than ours; and therefore, for God's sake, be good to us, for in you is all our trust.

And I beseech you, good master secretary, pray my lord my father and my lady to be so good to us, and to let me have their blessings and my husband their good will; and I will never desire more of them. Also, I pray you, desire my lord of Norfolk and my lord my brother to be good to us. I dare not write to them, they are so cruel against us; but if, with any pain that I could take with my life, I might win their good wills, I promise you there is no child living would venture more than I. And so I pray you to report by me, and you shall find my writing true, and in all points which I may please them in I shall be ready to obey them nearest my husband, whom I am most bound to; to whom I most heartily beseech you to be good unto, which, for my sake, is a poor banished man for an honest and a godly cause. And seeing that I have read in old books that some, for as just causes, have by kings and queens been pardoned by the suit of good folks, I trust it shall be our chance, through your good help, to come to the same; as knoweth the (Lord) God, who send you health and heart's ease. Scribbled with her ill hand, who is your poor, humble suitor, always to command,

Mary Stafford.

To the right worshipful and my singular good friend, Master Secretary to the king's highness, this be delivered."

Mary Boleyn could not warm the heart of the king who once loved her, though Queen Anne Boleyn managed to send money and a golden cup to help with expenses. Mary would never return from the countryside and probably did not see her sister again.

Chapter 7 – Anne Boleyn

The object of King Henry VIII's affections was born into a noble and wealthy family around the year 1501. Since no church records were kept of her birth, scholars disagree on the exact year and date, and the range of Anne's estimated birth year stretches from 1501 to 1507. She had a slightly older sister named Mary and a younger brother called George. Her father, Thomas Boleyn, had been one of King Henry VII's favorite linguists and diplomats and enjoyed many positions and titles under Henry VIII.

With their family background, it was natural that young Anne and Mary would be offered places at the English court to serve the Queen of England – Catherine of Aragon. As it happened, Anne would first join the French court before serving her own queen. When King Henry VIII's sister, Mary Tudor, was sent to France to marry the King Louis XII, Anne was required by her father Thomas to attend her in Paris. Only three months after the royal wedding, the elderly French king died. Mary Tudor secretly married her brother's good friend, Charles Brandon, and returned to England. Anne Boleyn did not accompany the royal party but stayed on at the French court in service to the teenaged Queen Claude.

In previous centuries it had been commonplace for queens and princesses to be accompanied by a staff of five to six noble ladies, but by the Tudor era that number had increased to at least a dozen. Noble girls like Mary and Anne would have been expected to join the court at the age of 12 or so, serving as junior maids before turning 16 and becoming a Maid of Honor. The term "lady-in-waiting" served as a generalization for the various jobs and titles of such servants. Their job was primarily to keep the queen company and make sure that she was never made to do anything resembling physical labor. The latter included dressing and undressing, using the lavatory by herself, bathing, and styling her hair. Ideally, a royal girl or woman would develop close friendships with her maids.

Anne had studied the usual subjects that a girl of her day was expected to study in England: Latin, singing, dancing, and music. Her education was considered good for a girl, but it expanded a great deal while she served for a year at the court of Margaret of Austria in a southern principality of the Netherlands. Margaret hired a tutor to help the young Anne Boleyn perfect her French skills, which served the girl well when she moved to Paris the next year. Margaret's court was very artistically-inclined, taking pleasure in fine paintings, music, and illustrated books. Anne was influenced greatly by her time in the Dutch principality, and she gained a love of art that would continue to grow in France. One of her favorite trends was the illuminated book. These books included the traditional blocks of text, surrounded by intricately drawn and colored borders, details, and illustrations on each page. Anne had her own books created in this style, as did many of her fellow courtiers.

In all, Anne Boleyn spent an estimated ten years in France. By the time she returned to the English court to serve Queen Catherine of Aragon in 1522, she was arguably more French than English. Anne's role at court was considered one of the greatest positions a noble lady could obtain. Though it was usually unpaid, ladies-in-waiting were given room and board. In particular, their presence at court gave Anne and Mary the chance to make friends with other upper-class ladies and meet potential husbands. Instead of finding bachelors, however, both girls became involved with the most ineligible man at the palace: the king.

Before he divorced Queen Catherine of Aragon, King Henry VIII had an affair with Mary Boleyn. Henry's love of flirtation and mistress-taking was well-known, and if a lady accepted his advances she could expect gifts and elevated ranking. Mary enjoyed the king's attention for some time before his wandering eye caught Anne, at which point he made up his mind to seduce the younger Boleyn girl.

As a young, attractive, and worldly noble girl, Anne became a popular member of the English court. She became engaged to her cousin James Butler at the will of her family, but the two rarely spoke although they were both at court. Anne fell in love with the Lord of Northumberland, Henry Percy, and the two of them decided to marry despite the wishes of Anne's family.

Noble marriages required the consent of the king, and when Henry VIII heard of Percy's intentions to wed Anne he refused outright. Soon afterward, the king began to pursue Anne for himself. For her part, Anne rejected – politely – the first advances of the king. She returned his gifts of jewelry and replied to his letters saying that she did not wish to be his mistress. Henry persevered for more than a year, writing letter after letter to the object of his affection while plotting to rid himself of Queen Catherine:

"MY MISTRESS & FRIEND,
my heart and I surrender our-
selves into your hands, beseeching
you to hold us commended to your
favour, and that by absence your
affection to us may not be lessened:
for it were a great pity to increase
our pain, of which absence produces
enough and more than I could ever
have thought could be felt, reminding us of a point in astronomy
which
is this: the longer the days are, the
more distant is the sun, and nevertheless the hotter; so is it with our
love, for by absence we are kept a
distance from one another, and yet
it retains its fervour, at least on my

side; I hope the like on yours, assuring you that on my part the pain of absence is already too great for me; and when I think of the increase of that which I am forced to suffer, it would be almost intolerable, but for the firm hope I have of your unchangeable affection for me: and to remind you of this sometimes, and seeing that I cannot be personally present with you, I now send you the nearest thing I can to that, namely, my picture set in a bracelet, with the whole of the device, which you already know, wishing myself in their place, if it should please you. This is from the hand of your loyal servant and friend,

H.R."

Eventually, Anne relented and gave Henry an opening: She told him that she could not become romantically involved with him while he still had a wife. At that point, the king must have realized he would have to choose between a foreign princess or Anne Boleyn as his next wife. There has been much speculation by contemporary peers and historians about whether Anne's father had anything to do with the change in Anne's stance towards the king.

The girls' father, Thomas Boleyn, had a shrewd political mind and could clearly see the benefit to his family if his daughter were able to become the king's long-term mistress. Or, better yet, the mother to another son. It is possible that Thomas even had inside information about Henry VIII's secret plot to denounce Catherine as queen and replace her with a younger, potentially more fertile woman. The little remaining evidence from that time, however, seems to suggest otherwise. In a letter from Eustace Chapuys, France's ambassador to

England, to Charles V of France, the subject of Henry VIII's proposed marriage to Boleyn's daughter was touched upon:

"I must add that the said earl of Wiltshire has never declared himself up to this moment; on the contrary, he has hitherto, as the duke of Norfolk has frequently told me, tried to dissuade the King rather than otherwise from the marriage."

Though Anne Boleyn was loyal to her family, she was a relatively independent woman who made as many of her own decisions as possible. The most likely scenario is that Anne genuinely grew to love Henry Tudor as he loved her and agreed to marry him on her own terms.

Chapter 8 – The Reformation and Divorce

By the late 1520s, King Henry VIII had had enough of his marriage to Catherine of Aragon. He no longer consulted the queen for political or spiritual advice, nor did he visit her. He was cold and distant, focused only on his future with Anne Boleyn, whom he had decided to marry. Under the Catholic church, however, divorce or annulment could only be granted by the Pope. Henry set his team of lawyers and clergy to the task of convincing the sitting Pope that his marriage to Catherine had been unlawful, since Catholic doctrine stated that a man must not marry his brother's widow.

Of course, this issue had already been dealt with before Catherine and Henry were married. Catherine had sworn she and Arthur Tudor had not consummated their marriage and based on that statement she and Henry were granted a papal dispensation to go ahead with their own wedding. Now, Henry wanted to undo all of that.

Henry's decision was not taken as lightly as it may have seemed to Catherine; he had, in fact, come to believe that the lack of male heirs between him and his queen was due to the fact that he had unlawfully taken his brother's wife. This personal revelation changed the king's perception on his family and caused Catherine – and Mary – a great deal of pain. It was the first glimpse of a new piece of Henry VIII's character, one that would come to define him.

Henry and Anne waited six years to acquire permission to marry, while Catherine fought desperately to change her husband's mind. She wrote to Pope Clement to plead her case, which convinced the latter to keep the royal couple's marriage intact. She also wrote to Henry, who would not speak to her face-to-face, and asked desperately what she had done to offend him so greatly.

Henry replied largely through his messengers and advisors, politely telling Catherine of his belief that their marriage was unlawful and unholy. He wished her no harm or ill but would not continue on as her husband.

On November 15, 1529, members of the court witnessed a heated argument between Henry VIII and Catherine of Aragon. Henry mentioned that due to the queen's having consummated her relationship with his brother Arthur, they could never have truly been married:

"The Queen replied that he himself, without the help of doctors, knew perfectly well that the principal cause alleged for the divorce did not really exist, 'cart yl l'avoit trouvé pucelle,' [translation: 'you found me to be a virgin'] as he himself had owned upon more than one occasion. 'As to your almoner's opinion in this matter,' she continued, 'I care not a straw; he is not my judge in the present case; it is for the Pope, not for him, to decide. Respecting those of other doctors, whether Parisian or from other universities, you know very well that the principal and best lawyers in England have written in my favour. Indeed, if you give me permission to procure counsel's opinion in this matter I do not hesitate to say that for each doctor or lawyer who might decide in your favour and against me, I shall find 1,000 to declare that the marriage is good and indissoluble.'"

Catherine was correct in her assumption that no lawyer or clergyman could find reason to annul her marriage to Henry. She was a much-loved and respected queen, and Henry's papal dispensation to remove her from his life would never come. In 1533, he stopped waiting for outside authority to vote in his favor and married Anne

Boleyn anyway. She was rumored to be pregnant and did indeed give birth to a healthy girl only a few months after the wedding. The baby was named Elizabeth Tudor.

Catherine was moved from Hampton Court Palace to her own dwelling, allowed to visit neither Henry nor their daughter Mary. Mary Tudor was declared illegitimate and therefore not an heir to the throne of England. Henry VIII asked Mary to swear an oath that her mother was not the Queen of England, which she refused to do. Young Mary was eventually embraced back into her father's life, but she would never see her mother again.

The marriage of Henry VIII to Anne Boleyn caused more than just a break in the king's first marriage. It also caused a break between England itself and the Catholic realm. In divorcing Catherine and marrying a second time, Henry had directly disobeyed the Pope and struggled to have his second marriage accepted throughout Europe. The king was prideful and sure of himself, however, and instead of pandering to his neighboring Catholic nations, he had the English Parliament declare him Head of the Church of England. As such, all religious doctrine, law, dispensations, and rituals were in the king's hands within his own kingdom.

Catherine continued to sign letters "Catherine the Quene" and thought Henry's heretical marriage to Anne was nonsense. She wrote him often and seemed worried for the state of his soul. She prayed for him and advised him to do the same. As for herself, she prayed for the reinstitution of her daughter Mary into the line of succession so that her life would be filled with the comforts and rights befitting a Princess of England.

The deposed queen became very sick soon after she was turned away from the palace she shared with Henry. At Kimbolton Castle in Cambridgeshire, Catherine grew weak and isolated. She stopped receiving most visitors except for close friends who could exchange her and Mary's letters. Three years after being officially demoted to Dowager Princess of Wales, which had been her English title after the death of Arthur Tudor, Catherine of Aragon asked for early communion from the Bishop of Llandaff and prayed ceaselessly until her death on January 29, 1536. Surgical procedures performed during Catherine's embalming revealed a black mass attached to her heart that may have been indicative of advanced cancer.

She was buried in Peterborough Cathedral, her funeral not attended by Mary or Henry VIII. To the end, Catherine believed herself to be the rightful Queen of England:

"In this world I will confess myself to be the king's true wife, and in the next they will know how unreasonably I am afflicted."

Chapter 9 – The Marriage and Death of England's Protestant Queen

King Henry VIII is believed to have proposed to Anne Boleyn in 1527. He waited for papal dispensation for a full six years before taking matters into his own hands. In January of 1533, Anne and Henry were married in secret. After the wedding, Henry's Parliament had little choice but to validate the marriage and name the king Head of the Church of England. Henry and Anne's kingdom was henceforth separate from the Catholic church.

The king wanted his new queen to be beloved by all of England and respected throughout Europe. To this end, he arranged a lavish, three-day coronation at the Tower of London for Queen Anne that began on May 29, 1533.

On the first day, Anne was dressed richly and taken from Greenwich Palace to the Tower via the River Thames. King Henry received her there with an assembly of London's political officials. A thousand guns were fired in her honor from the Tower, then some of the accompanying ships in the river followed suit. She stayed at the Tower that night with Henry before embarking on a royal procession through the city of London the next day. Her chariot was covered in silver cloth and all her ladies wore matching scarlet gowns; they paraded through the city and met with the Mayor of London, who presented Anne with a beautiful purse on behalf of himself and the residents of London. The procession carried on to the Palace of Westminster and Anne stayed there for the second night.

On the third day of her celebrations, Anne was finally brought to St. Peter's Abbey. The church was filled with Westminster monks, Lords of the Parliament, bishops, abbots, and every noble from the English court and surrounding area. Before Anne herself entered the Abbey, her crown and scepters were carried in by the Duke of Suffolk and two appointed earls. Anne walked under a golden canopy, wearing a crimson dress with purple velvet and ermine. Her brown hair was dressed in a coronet with gold and pearls.

The ceremony was officiated by the Archbishop of Canterbury and the Archbishop of York, with Anne Boleyn seated on an elevated throne in front of the altar. The congregation said Mass, then moved into Westminster Hall where the new queen was crowned and given the two scepters of her royal office. When the ceremony was finished and she was the official Queen of England, Anne was led by her father, Lord Wiltshire, to the celebratory feast. She sat on a high dais in front of several richly-laded tables and was served by various members of the nobility.

The kingdom was not as overwhelmed by Anne's charms as the king hoped. Despite all the pomp and circumstance of her coronation, the people of England were still quite loyal to Catherine of Aragon. They English did accept that Anne Boleyn was queen, however, which was more than could be said for the rest of Europe. In Spain, France, and the Holy Roman Empire, Catherine was still considered the official Queen of England, while Anne and King Henry were marked as heretics by a continent that was largely Catholic.

The new queen was considerably different than Catherine of Aragon had been. She was Protestant and supportive of the king's religious reformation; she was also younger and very interested in French arts and fashion. Anne's dresses featured pointed long sleeves and square necklines, and she preferred rounded French hoods to the sharply-angled English gable hoods. She made a point always to wear the color green and use pearls somewhere in her outfit, as they were her favorites. Many of her ladies-in-waiting began to use pearls as well as copy Anne's style of dress, which had been popular since she began to serve at court in 1522.

Fashion wasn't the only thing that changed at Henry's palace once Anne was formally installed there. She introduced French-style music and dancing at court and had many friends and courtiers join in with the new trend. Anne created dance steps of her own which she taught to her ladies and performed with them during parties.

Anne wasn't exactly warmly welcomed at home or abroad as the Queen of England, but she was confident in her marriage and acted the part splendidly. She was already pregnant when she married the king, and her first child was born September 7, 1533. The royal couple's first baby was a healthy girl, called Elizabeth Tudor. Over the course of the next three years, Anne became pregnant at least two more times, but both pregnancies ended in miscarriage or stillbirth. The last of these is believed by many to have occurred on the very day of Catherine of Aragon's funeral: January 29, 1536. The date of the miscarriage may have been a few weeks later, but in any case, the stillbirth was that of a male baby.

Though King Henry VIII was notoriously impatient regarding male heirs, his marriage to Anne was only three years old at that point and there were few serious signs that Anne was in danger. Nevertheless, he had taken notice of Jane Seymour while visiting her family home on business in 1533 and was clearly aware of her presence at court the following year in the service of Queen Anne.

While the Queen of England rested and recuperated from her miscarriage, the king became strict and decisive; he stated that Anne had used trickery to seduce him and he was finished with her. With Anne in her sick bed, completely ignorant of these events, Henry placed Jane Seymour in the royal apartments. Not even four months later Anne would be executed at the desire of her beloved husband.

Neither contemporary friends of Henry VIII nor world-class historians can interpret the king's exact reasons for having his queen's reputation ruined and her life ultimately ended, but there has been much speculation. The death of their unborn son is considered a primary factor behind Henry's treatment of the woman he changed England to wed, but so too is the meddling of Thomas Cromwell.

Thomas Cromwell had been a crucial figure in the plan to remove Catherine of Aragon from court and replace her with Anne Boleyn; he did not, however, remain loyal to his choice of queen. Cromwell and Anne were at odds when it came to the administrative rules of the new Church of England, mainly because Anne wanted church proceeds to be used for education and charity. Cromwell wanted to use the church money to grow the royal treasury – and of course, he wanted a percentage for himself. While the queen and Henry's closest advisor argued, the latter began plotting with the French ambassador, Eustace Chapuys, to rid the English court of Anne. It was hardly an unprecedented move on his part, though he did need Henry's approval to move swiftly.

In April, a musician named Mark Smeaton, employed by Anne Boleyn, was arrested on suspicion of having an affair with her. He denied the charge, however after having been imprisoned and tortured for some time, he confessed. A member of the nobility, Henry Norris, was arrested under the same charge, as were Sir Francis Weston, Sir Richard Page, and William Brereton. The most shocking arrest was that of George Boleyn, Anne's own brother. He was accused of incest and treason.

On May 2, 1536, Anne Boleyn herself was arrested and charged with treason against the king, though the charges were not explained to her. She was taken to the Tower of London via the River Thames, and once she was within the Tower she collapsed, immediately asking where her father and brother were, and what she was charged with.

A letter survives from the Tudor era that is said to be Anne's last message to Henry VIII, though its contemporary owner explained inaccuracies in the writing to the fact that it was copied by Cromwell:

"Sir, your Grace's displeasure, and my Imprisonment are Things so strange unto me, as what to Write, or what to Excuse, I am altogether ignorant; whereas you sent unto me (willing me to confess a Truth, and so obtain your Favour) by such a one, whom you know to be my ancient and professed Enemy; I no sooner received the Message by him, than I rightly conceived your Meaning; and if, as you say, confessing Truth indeed may procure my safety, I shall with all Willingness and Duty perform your Command.

But let not your Grace ever imagine that your poor Wife will ever be brought to acknowledge a Fault, where not so much as Thought thereof proceeded. And to speak a truth, never Prince had Wife more Loyal in all Duty, and in all true Affection, than you have found in Anne Boleyn, with which Name and Place could willingly have contented my self, as if God, and your Grace's Pleasure had been so pleased. Neither did I at any time so far forge my self in my Exaltation, or received Queenship, but that I always looked for such an Alteration as now I find; for the ground of my preferment being on no surer Foundation than your Grace's Fancy, the least Alteration, I knew, was fit and sufficient to draw that Fancy to some other subject.

You have chosen me, from a low Estate, to be your Queen and Companion, far beyond my Desert or Desire. If then you found me worthy of such Honour, Good your Grace, let not any light Fancy, or bad Counsel of mine Enemies, withdraw your Princely Favour from me; neither let that Stain, that unworthy Stain of a Disloyal Heart towards your good Grace, ever cast so foul a Blot on your most Dutiful Wife, and the Infant Princess your Daughter:

Try me, good King, but let me have a Lawful Trial, and let not my sworn Enemies sit as my Accusers and Judges; yes, let me receive an open Trial, for my Truth shall fear no open shame; then shall you see, either mine Innocency cleared, your Suspicion and Conscience satisfied, the Ignominy and Slander of the World stopped, or my Guilt openly declared. So that whatsoever God or you may determine of me, your Grace may be freed from an open Censure; and mine Offence being so lawfully proved, your Grace is at liberty, both before God and Man, not only to execute worthy Punishment on me as an unlawful Wife, but to follow your Affection already settled on that party, for whose sake I am now as I am, whose Name I could some good while since have pointed unto: Your Grace being not ignorant of my Suspicion therein.

But if you have already determined of me, and that not only my Death, but an Infamous Slander must bring you the enjoying of your desired Happiness; then I desire of God, that he will pardon your great Sin therein, and likewise mine Enemies, the Instruments thereof; that he will not call you to a strict Account for your unprincely and cruel usage of me, at his General Judgement-Seat, where both you and my self must shortly appear, and in whose Judgement, I doubt not, (whatsoever the World may think of me) mine Innocence shall be openly known, and sufficiently cleared.

My last and only Request shall be, That my self may only bear the Burthen of your Grace's Displeasure, and that it may not touch the Innocent Souls of those poor Gentlemen, who (as I understand) are likewise in strait Imprisonment for my sake. If ever I have found favour in your Sight; if ever the Name of Anne Boleyn hath been pleasing to your Ears, then let me obtain this Request; and I will so leave to trouble your Grace any further, with mine earnest Prayers to the Trinity to have your Grace in his good keeping, and to direct you in all your Actions.

Your most Loyal and ever Faithful Wife, Anne Bullen From my doleful Prison the Tower, this 6th of May."

All of the accused were found guilty, including the queen and her brother, and sentenced to be executed. According to existing law, a queen found guilty of adultery was supposed to be burned alive. Henry asked that Anne be beheaded instead, and had a special executioner brought in from France to do the job with a sword instead of the traditional axe. The day before Anne's execution was scheduled to take place, Thomas Cranmer pronounced the marriage between her and Henry Tudor void.

Anne climbed the scaffold on 19 May, 1536, dressed like a queen. She wore a dark grey damask gown with a scarlet petticoat underneath. Wearing a splash of vibrant, defiant red while facing execution was something Mary Start, Queen of Scots, and Marie Antoinette, Queen of France, would both do as well. Red, though to symbolize martyrdom, was a subtle way to show one's innocence in the face of death. Her hood, usually French, was a stiff English garment. She removed her ermine cape and headdress, tucked her hair into a small cap and allowed one of her maids to tie a blindfold in place. She knelt, prayed, and was killed with one stroke of the Frenchman's sword.

Chapter 10 – Mistress Mary Shelton

Mary Shelton was the youngest daughter of John and Anne Shelton, and one of 10 children who lived with their parents at Sheldon Hall in Norfolk. Her mother, Anne, was governess to Princess Mary Tudor, the king's first child by Catherine of Aragon. It was a strained relationship, since Shelton was under strict instructions not to let the little girl call herself "Princess" following the Reformation. Advisors to King Henry VIII did not want Mary to grow up to consider herself a royal, privileged heir. Anne was encouraged to physically punish young Mary if she referred to herself as a princess.

Anne's employment within the royal family was beneficial to all of her children. When her daughters became old enough, they were easily placed as ladies-in-waiting at the royal court. Mary, born sometime between 1510 and 1520, entered Henry Tudor's court to serve Queen Anne, the Protestant queen, soon after her marriage to Henry VIII. The young lady was thought to be a beautiful, well-read, and talented girl by her friends and peers. First cousins of the queen, her family were supporters of the Reformist movement, meaning that Mary understood much of the doctrine of the new Church of England. This could well have endeared her to the king, though it was likely her good looks and popularity that did the most to catch Henry's eye.

There is much confusion regarding the identity of Mary – and Margaret – Shelton. She appears either to have had a similarly-named sister, Margaret, or to have also been called Madge. Most historians concur that there were two Shelton girls, though it is difficult to say with conviction which was closest to King Henry. The most current research concludes that the girl in question was indeed Mary Shelton, while Margaret or "Madge" Shelton was closer to Queen Anne.

Mary was not only an avid reader, but a writer of poetry. She delighted in romantic verse and even worked together with other girls to create a book of poems and letters called the Devonshire Manuscript. This book was a collection of classic romantic writing copied out in full or excerpt, but it also contained new works allegedly by Mary Shelton, Margaret Douglas, and Mary Fitzroy, all of whom waited on Queen Anne Boleyn.

The Devonshire Manuscript was a huge success among Henry's courtiers, who enjoyed reading the verses as well as guessing who may have written the anonymous entries. The vivacious and exciting text most definitely came to the king's attention, since Henry loved literature and above all, romance. Mary's involvement in the popular book probably endeared the king even more to the attractive lady-in-waiting.

Some theories have gone so far as to suggest Anne Boleyn herself persuaded Mary to engage in a sexual relationship with King Henry VIII, apparently in an attempt of Anne's to put a sympathetic friend near the king. This theory may have some truth to it. By the time Mary and Henry began their affair, the king and queen's relationship had soured due to Anne's multiple miscarriages and Henry's constant cheating. As a friend and family member, Anne may have believed that it was better to have someone she could control in Henry's bed rather than a stranger. If this was indeed her strategy, it failed. Just a few months after Mary and Henry are said to have connected romantically, Anne Boleyn was put to death.

The executions of that spring seem to have put an end to Henry and Mary's relationship. There are no records available to suggest why their tryst came to a halt, but it was certainly a tumultuous time for everyone close to the king. Mary's sister, Margaret, suffered a great deal from the allegations made against her queen, since they also involved her fiancé. Henry Norris, an avid sportsman and close friend of King Henry, was likely matched with Margaret Shelton by the king himself. And yet, when the king needed his wife's reputation ruined, Norris was accused of adultery. He insisted that he was innocent, as did she, but both were found guilty and executed for adultery and treason in the spring of 1536.

It must have been a terrifying time for Margaret, and for her sister Mary as well. Though virtually all courtiers were at the mercy of King Henry's whims, she must have wondered if it would be better for her to pull away from Henry or encourage his desire. Perhaps he chose to end the affair himself, either because of her closeness to the queen or simply because his mind was occupied with so many other matters. It seems most likely that the king had decided to choose another woman for his next wife and was busy putting that plan into action.

It is difficult to say just how the execution of a woman Henry had clearly once loved affected the king, particularly because his behavior went on very much as usual throughout the entire year of 1536. His affair with Mary was not a new situation for the king, nor was his frustration with a queen who had delivered a girl and then suffered multiple stillbirths and miscarriages. It was, however, the first time the king was so desperate to rid himself of a wife that he actually had her accused and executed. This, like his fascination with the ladies-in-waiting at court, would prove to be another lifelong tendency.

Mary Shelton escaped the wrath of the king and his advisors, whereas many other women and men were not so lucky. Henry's fascination turned from her to Jane Seymour, another lady at court, and Mary was left mercifully without charge. Ten years after the execution of Queen Anne Boleyn, Mary Shelton married Sir Anthony Heveningham and the couple had five children together. At least one of her daughters, Abigail Heveningham, waited on Queen Elizabeth I in 1588. Her husband predeceased her, and Mary married for a second time in 1557 to Philip Appleyard. She and Heveningham are considered direct ancestors of Diana, Princess of Wales.

Chapter 11 – The Wooing of Jane Seymour

It was no secret that Henry VIII's new infatuation was Jane Seymour. In fact, this was mentioned in Anne Boleyn's last letter to her husband before he had her executed for treason. Indeed, the king had been romancing Anne's Maid of Honor for some time by the day of Anne's death, and this was so well known that Londoners sang rude rhymes about Jane and Henry's relationship. The king worried that his mistress would be insulted and scandalized by such things and immediately wrote to her on the subject:

"My dear friend and mistress,

The bearer of these few lines from thy entirely devoted servant will deliver into thy fair hands a token of my true affection for thee, hoping you will keep it forever in your sincere love for me. Advertising you that there is a ballad made lately of great derision against us, which if it go much abroad and is seen by you, I pray you to pay no manner of regard to it. I am not at present informed who is the setter forth of this malignant writing, but if he is found out he shall be straitly punished for it. For the things ye lacked I have minded my lord to supply them to you as soon as he can buy them. Thus hoping shortly to receive you in these arms, I end for the present your own loving servant and sovereign,

H. R."

Jane Seymour's estimated year of birth was 1509; the same year in which King Henry VIII was crowned. Like much of the nobility, Jane was related to the king via their common ancestor, King Edward III. Henry and Jane were fifth cousins; the latter was also distantly related to both Catherine of Aragon and Anne Boleyn. The middle daughter of ten children, Jane received a traditional education for a woman of her time. She knew how to read and write her own name, but nothing more. Instead of literature and history, like Queen Catherine, or arts and fashion, like Queen Anne, Queen Jane's interests were in domestic arts like embroidery and household organization.

Jane was so different from Queen Anne Boleyn, in fact, that it was said she was chosen by Henry because of her stark contrast to the deposed queen. She was never described as a beautiful girl, like all the others Henry took up with, but rather as meek, mild, pale, and plain. She was not the vivacious, headstrong girl that Anne had been, but a subservient mistress inclined to do as she was expected. Some even remarked that she seemed rather dull and unintelligent, but given Henry's charm, education, and intellect it seems unlikely that he would choose someone less than intuitive and insightful for a companion.

It is not possible to know exactly what was Jane Seymour's character, or what went through her mind during the whirlwind betrothal and marriage in 1536, but she must have immediately known when Henry's interest was piqued. Perhaps she did not know whether he intended to make her his mistress or wed her, but in either case she knew the potential pitfalls. To become Henry's mistress probably meant gifts of land and money as well as a quick marriage to someone friendly with the king. Becoming his queen, on the other hand, meant becoming responsible for producing a male heir – and if she proved incapable of such responsibility, suffering the ultimate price.

Jane Seymour probably acted according to what she believed was necessary to survive. After all, she was raised as a member of the reformed church and had served two Tudor queens before catching Henry's eye for herself. She had seen the failure of Catherine of Aragon's marriage, as well as the rushing highs and deadly lows of the marriage of Anne Boleyn. Jane was likely perfectly aware of what was needed of her as Henry's consort, and what could become of her if she did not act accordingly.

Jane's family may have done its own fair share of pushing Jane into the king's arms. The Seymours were an important family that was close to the crown. Knowing that Anne had fallen out of favour with Henry, Jane's father and brother believed they could provide the king with a new and better-suited match. The family crest, featuring a proud peacock, was suddenly changed to feature a phoenix. Clearly, the Seymours did not want anything resembling pride or assertiveness reflected on their pure, servile Jane. Many historians consider the swift replacement of Anne with Jane a coup on the part of the Seymours – a successful one whose remunerations would continue to flow long after the death of Jane herself.

King Henry found that Jane Seymour would not submit to his gifts and caresses for the same reason Anne had not – she would not become a mistress, but only a wife. It was a method that had worked for Anne Boleyn, and it worked once more for Jane. Most likely, King Henry believed that Jane's modesty was her own doing, and indeed this may well have been the case. It may also have been the advice of Jane's family, which she knew all too well was a good strategy.

Henry believed he was wooing Jane, but her family was probably equally wooing him! Of course, Jane herself had done most of the work in presenting herself as a modest and chaste lady simply because that's who she was. She had reached the age of 25 without having married or becoming caught up in an affair. The king assumed she was a virgin, and he was probably correct. The only scandal concerning Jane was actually the fault of her father, who had had an affair with his daughter-in-law. That scandal passed and if it did Jane any personal harm, it was not long-lasting.

When the king sent a gift of golden coins to his love interest, Jane is said to have knelt on her knees and begged the messenger to take them back. She told him that she was a virtuous maiden who could not accept gifts from a married man. She added that if the king wanted to make a gift of gold to her, it should perhaps be when she had attained an honorable marriage. Henry had heard that kind of talk before, and this time he didn't need to change the fundamental religious premise of his kingdom or wait for six years to follow through. The humility of his chosen lady was everything to him, just as it had been seven years before.

Once the reigning queen was thoroughly vanquished, Jane was at the mercy of King Henry's wishes, for good or ill.

Chapter 12 – Jane and the Prince

Jane Seymour and Henry VIII were married at the Palace of Whitehall, 11 days after Anne's execution. The ceremony took place in the Queen's Closet, which was actually a lush and well-appointed space among the official Queen's Rooms at the palace.

Henry gifted his new bride over a hundred properties but did not arrange for her coronation, allegedly due to the outbreak of plague in London. Gossip among courtiers insisted that Henry wouldn't bother to crown Jane until she provided him with a prince, and there may have been some truth to the rumor. It was also true that during the summer, the royals tended to leave England's capital city due to plague flare-ups, and thus it makes sense that the new queen should not spend time in the heat of the infected city. Despite not having an official coronation ceremony, Henry's third wife was formally pronounced queen on June 4, 1536.

Soon after the wedding, the king received disheartening news: his only son, Henry Fitzroy, had died from tuberculosis at the age of seventeen. Fitzroy and Henry were close; the king had been considering marriage arrangements for his illegitimate son since his birth. For many years, it appeared that young Fitzroy would be Henry's only male candidate for the succession – at least, the only illegitimate candidate whom the king condescended to recognize as his own. It was a difficult year for King Henry VIII, but the stresses the king suffered were surely compounded onto his new wife. Jane must have felt more responsibility than ever to give the king children as soon as possible.

Unlike her predecessor, Jane Seymour was not pregnant at the time of the marriage, nor did she become pregnant until the next year. Finally, an impending birth was announced in January 1537 and the baby was delivered safely on the 12th of October. It was a healthy boy and the instant heir to the throne of England. They named him Edward and named him Prince of Wales,

During those long first months of Jane and Henry's marriage, while they undoubtedly tried to conceive, Jane made an effort to reach out to the king's existing children. She was already very sympathetic to Mary and her mother Catherine of Aragon and wanted to find a way to reunite the girl and her sister, Elizabeth, with their father. Her timing was ideal, as far as Mary was concerned, because she was sick, weak, and worried that she might be next on the scaffold. At the end of June, Mary Tudor signed a court document stating that her mother was never the lawful Queen of England, and that she would follow the laws of her father, Henry VIII, to the letter. It was very difficult for Mary to sign any such statement, but by 1537 she had held out for nearly five years. At the age of 21, Mary Tudor needed the love of her father so that she could re-join the royal court, be married, and claim her allowance.

Jane wanted both Mary and Elizabeth to be reinstated as royal heirs to Henry's crown – after any of her own children, of course. While she did not succeed in convincing the king to recognize his daughters as potential heirs, she did convince him to welcome them into his home on several occasions. It was the beginning of a long-winded mending of a deep familial rift. This was especially important for Elizabeth Tudor, whose mother was killed by her father's order. It is possible that Jane was concerned for the safety of Anne's only child, which prompted her to soothe Henry's temper in reference to the young girl. Henry seemed satisfied to keep both daughters alive and well-cared for and he included them in more royal events. The two girls were present at their half-brother's christening and held the train of the baby's gown.

Unfortunately for Jane, delivering Prince Edward was a very painful and exhausting two-day process. She remained in bed while preparations were made for Edward's christening at the Chapel Royal on the 15th of October. King Henry organized an unforgettable event for his new son and had the christening font raised up so everyone in attendance could see the prince. The ceremony was performed by Archbishop Thomas Cranmer and at its end little Edward was pronounced Prince Edward, Duke of Cornwall and Earl of Chester.

Cranmer, Charles Brandon, and several other men highly-regarded by the king stood as Edward's Godfathers; the king's daughter Mary stood as his Godmother. There is some confusion as to whether or not Queen Jane actually participated in part of the christening ceremony, though most sources agree she did not venture from her bedroom and the boy was returned to her afterward.

Jane's physical state deteriorated, improved, then worsened again over the course of the next nine days. Modern doctors and historians can only guess what may have caused her illness, but many agree that Henry's third wife suffered from puerperal fever: a sickness related to childbirth in which the mother develops a severe uterine infection. Whatever the exact reason, Jane died on the 24th of October, not even two weeks after the birth of her son. Henry gave her a large funeral and buried her at St. George's Chapel in Windsor Castle, where he would later be interred.

Jane Seymour, Henry VIII's wife for just short of one year and six months, is the only one of the king's wives whom Henry actively mourned. The king was reportedly devastated at her death and wore black well into the next year. Henry's companions noted that he took up needlepoint after his wife's demise, which had been a great hobby of hers. It was a commemorative act that both memorialized Jane and connected Henry to her in his time of sorrow. Many of Jane's embroidered creations, including sleeve cuffs and pillows, were kept in the royal collection as long as a century after her death.

After Jane's death on October 24, 1537, the king only halfheartedly discussed other potential marriages. Henry wanted Jane to be remembered, cherished, and respected properly as the mother of the heir to England's throne, Prince Edward, and he made sure to keep her memory alive at court through paintings, embroidery and pointed references. The updated bird on the Seymour crest came to be particularly apt.

Her epitaph reads:

> *"Here lies Jane, a phoenix*
> *Who died in giving another phoenix birth.*
> *Let her be mourned, for birds like these*
> *Are rare indeed."*

Chapter 13 – Two Years a Widower

1537 was an emotional year for King Henry VIII. In January, he sustained a frightening concussion and leg injury which nearly killed him. His love of jousting was lost to him for the rest of his life, as was his formerly active lifestyle. He'd fallen out of love and instigated the downfall of a woman he once cherished so much that he broke with the very head of the Catholic Church. Reginald Pole had been sent from Rome to rally a war-cry against heretical England, and Henry Fitzroy, the king's illegitimate but well-loved son, was dead.

From October 1537 to January 1540, King Henry remained unmarried. It was the longest period of time in his adult life that he was without a wife. These particular years were also difficult because of the growing pains of the Church of England. Now that his personally-headed church had been established and its basic rules laid out, the world's first English-language Bibles had been written and distributed throughout the country. More people than ever before had different opinions about what the gospels truly meant, while priests and clergymen struggled to understand exactly what the king regarded as heretical. Henry had a lot on his plate, and perhaps with his son Prince Edward safely tucked away in the palace, he found the time in his bachelorhood to fully address other issues besides the succession.

Despite his genuine melancholy at the death of Jane, Henry knew that it was in his best interest to marry and ally himself with a powerful family or country. He was back on the marital market by 1538, mostly for political reasons, but did not marry until the beginning of 1540. He'd begun to put on a huge amount of weight due to his inactivity, the pain in his legs, and his constant eating, but this did not make the King of England any less attractive in the political sense. There were many available matches both at home and abroad, but no one in particular seemed fit to fill Jane's place by his side.

Henry spoke of marriage but did not focus on it for at least six months following the birth of Prince Edward. In fact, Henry turned his attention to the infant and made every effort to keep the tiny prince healthy and safe. He insisted that the boy's residence be kept impeccably clean so as to lessen the risk of disease and illness, asking that the servants in attendance wash the rooms and the prince's belongings according to instructions very strict for the time period. The little boy had everything a tiny child could want and much more, as his father installed him in his own formal household headed by members of the Seymour family. It was just as it had been for Henry Fitzroy, but much more fastidious in terms of security.

The same year that Jane Seymour died, Hans Holbein the Younger completed his iconic painting of King Henry VIII. The portrait is still the most well-known likeness of King Henry, depicting the overweight monarch as a stout and strong, broad-shouldered man of physical greatness. His posture, fists at his hips and feet planted firmly apart, shows intensity and confidence. The robes are finely-sewn, the codpiece large and the calf muscles the king was always so proud of were thick and well-defined. Though Henry may have been as large as 300 pounds by that time, the portrait seems to only hint at a broadness of the body with a well-placed coat and fur trim. It is a masterpiece in that Holbein managed to allude to Henry's great size without displeasing the subject. The painting, though lost in a 17th-century fire, was copied numerous times by other contemporary artists

Throughout 1538, the king was in discussions with German envoys and councils interested in writing out a treaty. At first uninterested, Henry decided to look into the matter further and invited his guests to take part in long, detailed forums about the finer points of his true religion. Talks continued into the next year, when Henry sent his own envoy to Cleves to seek the alliance of the Duchy's new ruler, William.

Thomas Cromwell, King Henry's most trusted advisor, remained very eager to transform England into a fully Protestant state. He had helped arrange Henry's marriage to Anne Boleyn on the premise that by doing so, England would enter a new religious age. Cromwell's continued push for reform had begun to irritate the king, but Henry's displeasure did nothing to dissuade the chief minister's scheming. Cromwell wanted to reconnect King Henry to the other European Protestant nations, which were few but not insignificant. To this end, he searched out potential brides from the continent.

The Duchy of Cleves, situated in the territory of the Holy Roman Empire, was a singularly Protestant region under the ultimate rule of a staunch Catholic ally. It was small but fierce and there were two girls within its lands who were noble enough to become Queens of England. When King Henry had had enough of bachelorhood, Cromwell pointed him in the direction of the Cleves family.

In the early part of 1540, King Henry enacted strict legislation against remaining Catholic monasteries in England and Ireland. Shap Abbey, Dunstable Priory, Bolton Abbey, Thetford Priory, and Waltham Abbey were all closed down due to the Dissolution of the Monasteries Act. It was huge progress for the Church of England but just as much of a loss for England's large population of traditional Catholics. The latter saw King Henry as a tyrant, while the former applauded his strong hand in shutting down and essentially looting the monasteries throughout the nation.

Despite this move, Henry remained unsure about just how far he wanted to go in terms of changing England's religious practices. He had been raised a devout Catholic and therefore hesitated to embrace full Protestantism, in spite of seeming to do so only seven years earlier. Instead, the king searched for a sort of medium-ground between the drastic reforms of Protestant Europe and the fully-Catholic traditions of his youth.

His choice of bride on January 6, 1540, was telling.

Chapter 14 – Anne of Cleves

Anne La Marck, better-known by her House name of Cleves, was 24 years Henry VIII's junior. She was born September 22, 1515, in the Duchy of Cleves which was inherited by her father, Johann III La Marck. She and her younger sister, Amalia, were both under serious consideration for the vacant position of Queen of England in 1539. For the king's fourth wife, Henry's Chief Minister was interested in a foreign queen; the Duchy of Cleves was an independent state of the Holy Roman Empire, now part of modern Germany.

Anne grew up in Schloss Burg, a beautiful castle near the city of Solingen, with three siblings: Amalia, Sybil, and Wilhelm. Upon the death of Johann III in 1558 (or 1559, depending which sources are correct), Wilhelm inherited the Duchy of Jülich-Cleves-Berg and conducted his property under many of the ideals of the European Reformation; he was a member of the Schmalkaldic League, a union of Protestant states against the Holy Roman Emperor.

Anne was not formally educated, but she knew how to read and write in German and was considered an attractive and gentle young woman by most nobles from nearby Duchies and neighboring nations. She enjoyed playing cards and made efforts to be an enjoyable conversationalist; she was also very skilled at contemporary domestic duties such as sewing and embroidery. Unlike most noble women in England, Anne of Cleves learned no foreign languages, nor was she taught to sing or play an instrument.

Like all members of European royal families, Anne of Cleves was subject to the whims of her parents when it came to marriage. At the young age of ten, she was engaged to Francis, heir to the Duchy of Lorraine, but this arrangement was canceled in 1535.

Six years after Henry VIII had reformed England's religion, Cromwell and some of his top Protestant advisors began to feel the king was less enthusiastic about Protestantism than he had been in past years. It also appeared that France and the Holy Roman Empire were conspiring to invade anti-Catholic England, which doubly prompted Thomas Cromwell to seek Henry's new wife from a fellow Protestant state. The youngest daughters of the Duchy of Cleves were selected as the most appropriate brides for King Henry VIII, so the king sent his court portraitist, Hans Holbein the Younger, to create likenesses of both girls.

Holbein created a beautiful portrait of Anne wearing the puffed, wide sleeves and high-waisted skirt of German style, as well as the isolated style of headdress traditional in her part of Europe. The young woman made a lovely portrait that showed off her symmetrical facial features, classically well-balanced figure and pleasant facial expression. Focused entirely on Anne's upper body, however, the portrait failed to show the lady's height and size. She was a tall and robust woman – still considered very attractive by many, but not within King Henry VIII's normal taste.

Holbein also created a rudimentary sketch of Anne's sister, Amalia, wearing very similar clothing and accessories. Amalia had a thinner, perhaps longer face than Anne. It was ultimately Anne of Cleves' portrait that won Henry VIII's admiration, so Wilhelm arranged a marriage contract with the King of England and sent his sister to Henry's court.

By the time Anne was ready to travel to England, the short-lived peace between the Holy Roman Empire and France was growing unreliable. It was not safe for Anne to travel through either of these nations, but there was no other way to reach England from Cleves.

French King Francis I offered his support, while Charles V gave Anne a French passport that enabled her to travel through the Netherlands and depart the continent.

Ironically, the animosity between Francis I, Charles V, and England was a large part of the reason Henry VIII sought a Protestant alliance with the Duchy of Cleves in the first place; when the French and Holy Roman Empire decided to cooperate with Henry and Wilhelm, Henry lost his reason to wed Anne at all. The King of England was not unaware of this, but he'd agreed to marry the girl and he wanted to follow through on his promise. So, Anne of Cleves traveled westward in the heart of winter and arrived in England by New Year's Day of 1540.

As soon as his bride was within reach, Henry hurried to meet her – in costume, with eight of his privy councilors:

"On which day the kyng which sore desyred to see her Grace accompanyed with no more then viii. persons of his prevy chambre, & both he & they all apparelled in marble coates prevely came to Rochester, and sodainly came to her presence, which therwith was sumwhat astonied: but after he had spoken & welcomed her, she with most gracious & loving countenance and behaviour him received & welcomed on her knees, whom he gently toke up & kyssed: & all that after-noone commoned and devised with her, & that night supped with her, & the next day he departed to Grenewich , & she came to Dartford. [sic]"

Though Henry was every bit the gentleman during his impromptu meeting with his bride-to-be, his friends later stated that the king was in no way satisfied with the way Anne looked. This may have been true, but there is likely another reason why the king was not impressed by Anne. Appearing in disguise to the person you love was a tradition at court, whereby the person being visited is supposed to recognize their loved one or fall in love immediately.

Given the king's well-known ego, it's possible that he was insulted Anne didn't recognize him until he removed his disguise and his courtiers began to wait on him. Henry VIII was accustomed to his brides showing the utmost respect and attention to him; believing he was a servant of the king, Anne merely showed Henry politeness and then ignored him. After their meeting, rude rumors circulated concerning just what Henry had said about his bride-to-be. Nevertheless, the marriage went ahead on January 6, 1540, at the Palace of Placentia in Greenwich. The Archbishop Thomas Cranmer performed the ceremony.

Henry confessed to Thomas Cromwell the next day that he had not made love with his new wife and therefore the marriage was not yet official. Furthermore, the king could not say whether he would finalize the marriage at any point in the future. Anne, though 24 years of age, had never been married before and seemed not to understand this detail. She confessed to one of her Maids of Honor that the king bid her good morning and good night each day, kissing her hand sweetly; the latter assured the queen that much more was necessary to bring about a baby.

Anne of Cleves never consummated her marriage to King Henry VIII of England. After she was ordered to leave Henry's residence and go on her own to Richmond Palace, she discovered that her marriage was in trouble. She fainted, and when she recovered herself, Anne refused to agree to Henry's proposed annulment.

Chapter 15 – Annulment and Later Years

Anne of Cleves was hurt that she had displeased her husband so severely, so soon into their marriage, but once she had time to gather her thoughts, she knew better than to argue with someone with Henry VIII's reputation. Though at first, she insisted on knowing what she had done wrong, Anne soon realized it was best to agree to the annulment and make things easy on the king.

On the 9th of July, six months after their wedding, Henry and Anne of Cleves had their marriage annulled. Henry blamed the split on many things, including Anne's looks, his disbelief in her virginity, her canceled betrothal to Francis of Lorraine, and mostly, Thomas Cromwell. The latter was executed for treason mere weeks after Anne of Cleves was turned out of Henry's palace and given her own collection of English residences.

She wrote to him on July 11 and expressed her desire to do as he willed:

"Pleaseth your most excellent majesty to understand that, whereas, at sundry times heretofore, I have been informed and perceived, by certain lords and others of your grace's council, of the doubts and questions which have been moved and found in our marriage; and how hath petition thereupon been made to your highness by our nobles and commons, that the same might be examined and determined by the holy clergy of this realm; to testify to your

highness by my writing, that which I have before promised by word and will, that is to say, that the matter should be examined and determined by the said clergy; it may please your majesty to know that, thought this case must needs be most hard and sorrowful unto me, for the great love which I bear to your most noble person, yet, having more regard to God and his truth than to any worldly affection, as it beseemed me, at the beginning, to submit me to such examination and determination of the said clergy, whom I have and do accept for judges competent in that behalf. So now being ascertained how the same clergy hath therein given their judgment and sentence, I knowledge myself hereby to accept and approve the same, wholly and entirely putting myself, for my state and condition, to your highness' goodness and pleasure; most humbly beseeching your majesty that, though it be determined that the pretended matrimony between us is void and of none effect, whereby I neither can nor will repute myself for your grace's wife, considering this sentence (whereunto I stand) and your majesty's clean and pure living with me, yet it will please you to take me for one of your most humble servants, and so to determine of me, as I may sometimes have the fruition of your most noble presence; which as I shall esteem for a great benefit, so, my lords and others of your majesty's council, now being with me, have put me in comfort thereof; and that your highness will take me for your sister; for the which I most humbly thank you accordingly.

Thus, most gracious prince, I beseech our Lord God to send your majesty long life and good health, to God's glory, your own honour, and the wealth of this noble realm.

From Richmond, the 11th day of July, the 32nd year of your majesty's most noble reign.

Your majesty's most humble sister and servant,

ANNE, THE DAUGHTER OF CLEVES"

For accepting his offer of marital annulment, King Henry VIII rewarded Anne of Cleves richly. If she worried that her life was in danger, she needn't have concerned herself; Upon their annulment, Henry gave his fourth wife Richmond Palace, Bletchingley Manor, Chelsea Old Manor and Anne Boleyn's childhood home, Hever Castle. He also gave her a comfortable annual salary and let her keep all the jewels, clothing, furniture, and other small property she had amassed during her short time as his wife.

Most prestigiously, Anne was granted the right to be called "Sister of the King." Thereafter, she was officially treated as a member of the royal family. Without a doubt, Anne of Cleves was the luckiest of all Henry VIII's wives. She neither died in childbirth, nor at the executioner's block, nor in isolation and sickness as had Catherine of Aragon. Instead, she flourished under the influence of the king and his lavish gifts.

After the marriage was ended, Anne decided to continue living in England, but stayed mostly out of the public eye. She chose Hever Castle, in Kent, as her regular home, and received King Henry there on multiple occasions. The two grew to be true friends, so much so that it was eventually rumored Henry would marry Anne a second time. This was untrue, but as the King's sister, Anne was often invited to court and received happily by Henry.

Among Anne's regular guests at Hever Castle were the Princesses Elizabeth and Mary. Both girls developed a close relationship with their former stepmother, particularly the like-minded Elizabeth. The younger princess was a faithful Protestant, having grown up entirely in the era of the Church of England, and her religious beliefs were perfectly in line with Anne's own. Mary was not spiritually likeminded, as her loyalty had always secretly lain with her mother's Catholic faith. When she inherited the throne in 1553, Mary's bloody reign spared few people: Anne of Cleves would be one of that lucky minority.

It was likely Anne's intelligence and positive that not only saved her life but gave her more luxury than she could comprehend. After her death on July 16, 1557, Anne of Cleves was given a full royal funeral and burial at Westminster Abbey at the behest of Queen Mary I. She had outlived King Henry VIII and his five other wives and been an important example of kindness and pragmatism to young Elizabeth Tudor. Anne of Cleves lived to the age of 41 and died following a short illness that modern historians believe may have been cancer.

Chapter 16 – Catherine Howard

It should have surprised no one (except Anne of Cleves) that Henry VIII had another bride in mind when he decided to annul his marriage to Anne. True to form, Henry's choice was one of his wife's ladies-in-waiting: Catherine Howard.

It's difficult to tell what the teenaged girl looked like from her Hans Holbein the Younger portraits, because Henry's official court portraitist had a rather stiff and particular style. His painting of the young object of King Henry's desire makes Catherine appear much older and less charismatic than she truly was. Besides the girl's pale white skin and dark blonde hair, we know little of her true likeness.

The very young and vivacious Catherine Howard was only 15 or 16 years old when she married 49-year-old King Henry on July 28, 1540. Their wedding took place the same day Thomas Cromwell was beheaded, which had been a somewhat shocking development in the king's council. It marked a new beginning for the king, who likely felt the effects of aging more acutely than ever and wanted to embrace new blood in his personal life as well as in the Privy Council.

Catherine Howard grew up in the care of her father's stepmother, the Dowager Duchess of Norfolk. It was normal for the daughters of poor nobility to live with a distant relative, in this case in the company of other girls with the same background. The duchess was responsible for teaching the girls in her care how to conduct themselves in the company of other nobles, including royalty, so that they might make excellent marital matches when the time came.

Not every young ladies' home quite delivered on this promise, and Catherine Howard's most certainly did not. Young Catherine and many of her friends at the estate were in the habit of sneaking their male friends into the bedroom late at night and staying up until the early hours flirting, gossiping, and falling in love. In 16th-century England, such behavior was beyond taboo. If discovered, it could ruin a girl's reputation for the rest of her life, not only preventing her from getting married and finding a comfortable situation but potentially breaking up any future marriage she did acquire.

In the bloom of youth and political innocence, Catherine and her friends simply enjoyed themselves and thought little of the consequences. Catherine herself had a serious romantic relationship with the secretary of the household, Francis Dereham. The two of them saw each other on a daily basis, and while Francis was away from the estate he left Catherine in charge of his household, belongings, and money. Completely in secret, the young couple agreed to marry one another as soon as it became possible. Unfortunately, the Duchess found out about their arrangement and immediately fired Dereham.

As supposedly inappropriate as Catherine's relationship was with Francis, it had the merit of being consensual. The same cannot be said for other so-called romantic affairs she would eventually be blamed for – in particular, the sexual relationship with her music teacher, Henry Mannox. This took place while Catherine was in the care of the Duchess, but before Francis Dereham joined the household. Though Mannox presented a case in which his student flirted with him and enjoyed herself, the girl told a slightly different story. In Catherine's opinion, Mannox had imposed upon her when she was only a young girl and she let him do what he liked, knowing little better.

Dereham and Howard, for their part, lovingly referred to each other as husband and wife, but their agreement was betrayed by the Duchess. Francis departed for Ireland and probably never saw Catherine again.

In 1539, Catherine moved into her uncle's house close to London and met a cousin of her mother's, Thomas Culpeper. Culpeper was one of King Henry VIII's Privy Chamber Gentlemen, meaning that he had access to the king's personal rooms as a body servant. Thomas was young, handsome and relatively important, which immediately impressed Catherine. Soon after this meeting, Catherine was given her own position at court as a lady-in-waiting to Queen Anne of Cleves. Almost immediately upon her arrival, Catherine was noticed by the king. In less than a year, the two were married and the new queen was happily installed in her own royal apartments.

It was a joyous time for Queen Catherine Howard, who had little to do but buy beautiful French gowns bedecked with expensive jewels and adornments. The couple left London in the heat of August to avoid plague season, and Henry entertained himself by lavishing the young queen in luxury everywhere they traveled. She had all the dresses, jewelry, and beautiful things she wanted, plus the best food and drink, and the king's indulgence in her relatively childish behavior. Though the king was aging, overweight, and in a great deal of pain from the ulcers on his legs, he enjoyed watching the little queen play with her friends in the dirt or chasing each other about the various royal estates.

One of Catherine's great joys was to meet 7-year-old Elizabeth Tudor, since the two were cousins through the Boleyn family. The new queen made sure to have Elizabeth sitting across from her or beside her at every meal when they were in the same palace. Her admiration was requited, and Elizabeth very much enjoyed spending time with her third stepmother and receiving little gifts from her.

After the plague died down along with the heat, Henry continued his liberal spending, this time on the Palace of Whitehall and a memorable Christmas celebration at Hampton Court Palace that same year. Queen Catherine received diamonds, furs, and pearls from the king on one of his most treasured holy days. Though often moody from the pain he suffered, King Henry did everything in his power to make 1540 an especially enjoyable year for himself and his little bride. He went so far as to have a special gold crown coin minted in honor of his latest marriage.

In the first part of 1541, the courtiers began to look for signs of pregnancy in Queen Catherine. It was determined that once she was with child, she would have her official coronation celebration. Unfortunately, peers from the queen's past began to appear at the palace, asking favors from Catherine in return for their silence about her relationships with Dereham and Mannox. She had little choice but to do as they asked, and soon her position at King Henry's court was teetering on the precipice of disaster.

Chapter 17 – The Culpeper Affair

Catherine Howard had already fallen in love with Thomas Culpeper by the time King Henry gave her any notice, and this was not something that marrying the king could change. Where a more mature woman would have known to use the utmost discretion in her personal life after entering into a marriage with Henry VIII, Catherine Howard either didn't understand this importance or she simply could not help but follow her young heart.

Catherine and Thomas had exchanged letters and spent time together at court before the former became betrothed, and even considered marrying each other. It would have been a fine match; they were of a suitable age, members of the English nobility, and even came from the same family. Moreover, Thomas and Catherine had a mutual affinity for one another, which Catherine surely could not have had for the aged, obese, sickly King Henry. Nevertheless, one does not turn down a marriage proposal from a king, even if said king has murdered a previous wife.

At some point after the royal wedding, the new queen began receiving visits from Thomas Culpeper in her private rooms. One of her most trusted Maids of Honor, Jane Boleyn, would sit outside in the hall and make sure the couple wasn't discovered. For many months, Catherine's affair eluded the king and his councilors, but the situation became impossible to control once the queen's old peers began making demands of her.

By the autumn of 1541, many of these very extortionists had been appointed to positions in Catherine's employment so as to keep them satisfied and quiet. They were not particularly inclined to remain silent, however, and soon the queen's secrets became known to Thomas Cranmer. The Archbishop immediately took it upon himself to research the allegations against Catherine and soon presented the king with a warrant for her arrest and trial. Among many confessions, Cranmer had located a letter in the queen's handwriting in Culpeper's bedchamber:

"Master Culpeper,

I heartily recommend me unto you, praying you to send me word how that you do. It was showed me that you was sick, the which thing troubled me very much till such time that I hear from you praying you to send me word how that you do, for I never longed so much for a thing as I do to see you and to speak with you, the which I trust shall be shortly now.

That which doth comfortly me very much when I think of it, and when I think again that you shall depart from me again it makes my heart die to think what fortune I have that I cannot be always in your company.

Yet my trust is always in you that you will be as you have promised me, and in that hope I trust upon still, praying you that you will come when my Lady Rochford is here for then I shall be best at leisure to be at your commandment, thanking you for that you have promised me to be so good unto that poor fellow my man which is one of the griefs that I do feel to depart from him for then I do know no one that I dare trust to send to you, and therefore I pray you take him to be with you that I may sometime hear from you one thing.

I pray you to give me a horse for my man for I had much ado to get one and therefore I pray send me one by him and in so doing I am as I said afor, and thus I take my leave of you, trusting to see you shortly again and I would you was with me now that you might see what pain I take in writing to you.

Yours as long as life endures

Katheryn.

One thing I had forgotten and that is to instruct my man to tarry here with me still for he says whatsomever you bid him he will do it."

It was difficult to argue that the letter had been forged, since Catherine was not very skilled at writing and her hand was easy to identify. Catherine was arrested, as were Thomas Culpeper, Francis Dereham, and Henry Mannox. On the 24th of November, 1541, the queen was imprisoned at Syon Abbey, Middlesex. Cranmer told the king that upon questioning, Catherine was in a such a frenzied state of terror that he found it necessary to remove everything from her room that she may use to harm herself. She would not see Henry again.

The king was furious. Henry's great love for Catherine Howard had been largely based on his perception of her as a youthful virgin, untouched by other men or the harshness of life. He called her the perfection of womanhood and believed that she was pure innocence personified. If he'd thought that Catherine's very tender age made her immune to the emotions, desires, and hardships of a fully-grown woman, he was wrong.

Catherine Howard testified that she had never been engaged to Francis Dereham, saying instead that he had raped her. She also stated that Henry Mannox took advantage of her young age but did not deny having a relationship with Thomas Culpeper before marrying King Henry VIII. As her letter was undated, the only proof that her statement concerning Culpeper was false came from the testimony of Jane Boleyn, the widow of Anne Boleyn's brother George. Jane had seen her husband and sister-in-law struggle with the very same accusation of adultery and treason in 1536 and she knew how the investigation was likely to turn out. Probably in an attempt to avoid torture and ultimately save herself, the Boleyn widow cooperated immediately with Cranmer. She, too, was arrested for complicity in treason.

Catherine Howard languished at Syon House until February 11, 1542, when she was taken to the Tower of London via the River Thames. The next day, she was told to prepare for her execution. She took advantage of the warning and asked to borrow the executioner's block so that she might practice how best to lay her head.

Stripped of her royal title, Catherine Howard climbed the steps of the scaffold looking very weak and fragile. She could not manage many words, probably due to sickness and fright, but she did tell those assembled how she deserved her fate for her trespasses against the king. She was executed on or near the same spot as Anne Boleyn had been six years earlier. It was the 13th of February. Thomas Culpeper had already been killed by the executioner's axe, and Francis Dereham hung, drawn and quartered. Henry Mannox received no punishment.

Chapter 18 – Katherine Parr

Katherine Parr was born to a noble northern English family whose roots stretched back to King Edward III. Her exact birth date is unknown but thought to be within the year 1512. She had two younger siblings, a father who was very close to King Henry VIII, and a mother who was a close companion of Queen Catherine of Aragon. In fact, Henry's first queen had been young Katherine's godmother.

The eldest Parr daughter had a lot of life to live before becoming Henry VIII's sixth and final wife. She grew up in Westmorland, receiving a typical education that consisted of some literature, music, needlework, and languages. Young Katherine was an eager student who had a particular penchant for languages, learning how to speak and write English, Latin, Italian, and French. She spent her formative years in King Henry VIII's Protestant England, which her father and mother supported. Protestantism would be a defining feature of Katherine's character, particularly after becoming acquainted with the king.

Katherine married at the age of 17 to a sickly man named Edward Burgh who was in his twenties. This first coupling would turn out to be a typical sort of marriage for Katherine, who married four times throughout her life. Not much is known about the unfortunate Edward Burgh, since he only lived another four years after the marriage and did not survive to inherit his father's title of Baron of Gainsborough. Katherine's duties in her first marriage were typical of a woman in her status: household management and the care of her chronically-ill husband.

Katherine's second marriage occurred in 1534, to John Neville, 3rd Baron Latimer. Though her husband was twice her age and had two children from previous marriages, Katherine was able to move into her own house with her new family and start fresh. Between husbands, she had been reliant on friends and family relations to offer housing and provisions for her. Such a predicament was quite usual for the Tudor era, if one was a woman. Like the vast majority of her female peers, Katherine needed a patron to keep her from abject poverty. John Neville would be her lifeline for nine years.

Life as a Latimer was not simple, though it was reasonably luxurious. The family lived at Snape Castle and was quite influential amongst English northerners, but that influence became a liability during the Lincolnshire Uprising in 1536. Though Lord Latimer himself was allied with King Henry – if not actually Protestant himself – his neighbors wanted to strong-arm Parliament into allowing them to keep their Catholic churches, customs, and laws. Outraged at the king's decision to marry Anne Boleyn and reform all of England under Protestantism, northern rebels forced Katherine's husband to join them in revolt or face the consequences. Latimer did so, leaving his wife and children at home alone.

Still quite a young woman, Katherine struggled to care for two step-children and herself while isolated at Snape Castle, wondering if her husband would be killed or bring the household into ruin. There was little hope of a good outcome during those tumultuous years. If the Pilgrimage of Grace, as the northern rebellion was called as it formed and moved south, was successful, northern England could be split from its southern half. If, on the other hand, the king took offense to the revolt, Latimer and all involved could be stripped of their titles and land, then tortured and killed by soldiers of the crown.

Katherine had been born in the south of England and her parents were in direct service of the crown, which meant that she had a better understanding of the Church of England than did older generations or those Catholic strongholds in the north. Latimer's chapel at Snape Castle was in the Catholic fashion, but the lady of the house was Protestant at heart. John Neville had no desire to call out King Henry on his religious reforms, and so in the guise of supporting the extremist faction that surrounded him, he acted as a diplomat between the protestors and the crown.

His wife must have been incredibly fearful during those long years without John, especially when Catholic rebels took her and the children hostage in exchange for John's return from London. The absent 3rd Baron Latimer returned and negotiated the release of his family. Hard-pressed by both sides of the rebellion, Latimer came under close scrutiny by Thomas Cromwell, King Henry VIII's foremost advisor. To the king and his council, it seemed likely that John Neville was just as much a rebellious conspirator as the rest of those involved in the Pilgrimage of Grace; to the rebels, Neville seemed to close to the king. It was a situation he barely escaped. When the charge of treason was given up, Latimer moved his family south.

Katherine's husband had dampened his reputation, and for this reason Thomas Cromwell was able to use him as a sort of errand boy over the next few years. When King Henry grew tired of Cromwell's presence and had him executed in 1540, life became easier for the Latimer family. John attended business at court in London from time to time, where Katherine visited her sister. By the time the reputation of the family had started to improve, John Neville became sick and had to rely on his wife to care for him as well as his children. She nursed him until his death in 1553.

Living in and near London those five or six years meant that Katherine had been introduced to many influential people at the king's court, including the king's daughter, Lady Mary. The two were close in age and they became fast friends, Katherine often visiting Mary at court. She also became introduced to Henry VIII's brother-in-law, Thomas Seymour. The two enjoyed one another's company to the extent that Katherine hoped they would marry. Before any such arrangement could be made, however, the thirty-year-old widow came to the attention of the king himself. Henry, never satisfied with or without a wife, decided Katherine was the perfect candidate to become his sixth queen. Like her predecessors, Katherine had little choice but to agree to the king's proposal. After all, Thomas Seymour would never pursue her while she had the king's eye, and Henry was nothing if not persistent.

By 1543, King Henry VIII was 52 years old and not at all healthy. His weight had ballooned to over 300 pounds, his legs were full of infection that leaked and stank; he spent as little time as possible on his feet. It's entirely possible that Henry had witnessed the kind ministrations of Lady Latimer to her ill and dying husband for several years, and now he wanted that patience and kindness for his own benefit. He married Katherine on July 12, 1543.

Having twice been a wife, and stepmother to two children, Katherine was a practiced hand at matrimony. She was careful, sweet, patient, and caring, all qualities that appealed to Henry in his senior years. Furthermore, the king's sixth wife was genuine in her adoration of the new faith, which had kept her safe in the south of England while Catholics terrorized her in the north. Henry and Katherine bonded over their shared religious beliefs, talking about the finer points of the Church of England privately for hours. In those years, Henry's church was not formally known as Protestant, as there were variants between his religious laws and the laws of other Protestant nations. Though Katherine seemed a happily full-fledged Protestant, she had to defer to Henry's specifications concerning religious practices.

Unlike the women who came before her, Katherine Parr was neither expected to be virginal nor produce children. She was there to be a sweet and loving wife, a role at which she knew how to excel. She took care to have her stepdaughter, Margaret Neville, installed as one of her ladies-in-waiting, and did the same for her stepson's wife. As for her three new stepchildren, Katherine made haste to become better acquainted with them and see that they had the mothering and education they deserved.

Princess Mary and Katherine were already friends; however Princess Elizabeth and Prince Edward were only ten and six years old, respectively. Elizabeth had just lost yet another stepmother in Catherine Howard and was old enough to truly feel the succession of losses in this respect. Edward had just reached the age at which his formal education was to begin, which meant a great deal of household administration awaited Katherine upon moving into Hampton Court Palace.

For Henry, this last marriage functioned much like his first. He and his wife were friends, and he trusted her. They sat together regularly, she in his lap or he with his sore legs in hers while she massaged them. Henry listened to Katherine when she spoke about the goodness of his daughters and the importance of reinstating their names into the royal succession. Remembering the same advice from Jane Seymour, the wife he'd treasured since her delivery of Prince Edward, the king finally wrote Elizabeth and Mary back into his will as legitimate daughters.

Having helped Mary and Elizabeth achieve their legitimacy, Katherine turned to the work of educating little Edward. He was a smart boy with a head for finance and military tactics, and his stepmother made sure he learned all he could of Protestantism, history, and language. Even she continued her own education alongside Edward and Elizabeth, taking up Spanish as well as theology. The younger royal children bonded with Katherine as one of their main tutors; it was a time that both Elizabeth and Edward would remember for the rest of their lives.

In 1544, Henry VIII brought his armies to France in another attempt to take back England's lost property there. Upon leaving England, the king did something he hadn't done since Catherine of Aragon was alive: he made the queen regent in his place.

Katherine was admired by Thomas Cranmer, her own uncle, and well-liked by the other members of her Regency Council; the queen ruled easily and as she pleased during the three months Henry was abroad. Though the king returned without victory in France, Katherine knew she'd earned his continued trust and respect.

The queen's confidence in her position grew after the French campaign, and she began to publish her own books on theology, such as *Psalms or Prayers*. These were notably the very first books published in England that had been written by a woman – at least in her own name. Katherine's writing and philosophical prowess, coupled with her solid command of the regency, must have made a lasting impression on both Mary and Elizabeth, who would both become future Queens of England.

The queen's blatant love of continental Protestantism earned her some enemies in the Privy Council, which was still partially constructed of die-hard Catholics whom Henry nevertheless trusted. After the death of Thomas Cromwell, Henry himself appeared to soften on religious reform. Taking advantage of the situation, the Bishop of Winchester and Lord Wriothesley made a case against the queen as a heretic and took it to the king. Katherine found a copy of the warrant and ran to see Henry as soon as she was sufficiently calm. She humbled herself before the king and lamented that she had spoken too much on the subject of theology without his approval. She apologized profusely and stroked her husband's ego desperately. Henry sent her back to her rooms.

She was spared in spectacular fashion. Henry, having already forgiven his wife for any perceived transgressions against his dogmatic religious doctrine, sought to teach his councilors a lesson. Soon after his wife's apology, the king took Katherine outside to enjoy the palace gardens. They were interrupted by Lord Wriothesley, who, not having been informed of the king's desire to overlook the heresy charges, attempted to arrest the queen for treason. Henry VIII struck the Lord and his attendants forcefully, sending them away and stating for all in earshot that his queen was not to be questioned.

Queen Katherine remained at her husband's side and was rebuked no more by anyone on his council. She continued to foster a loving relationship with the king's children, and on New Year's Day, 1545, Katherine received a religious book from Princess Elizabeth that the latter had translated into English herself:

"TO OUR MOST NOBLE AND virtuous queen KATHERINE,

Elizabeth her humble daughter wisheth perpetual felicity

and everlasting joy.

NOT ONLY knowing the affectuous will and fervent zeal, the which your highness hath towards all godly learning, as also my duty towards you (most gracious and sovereign princess) but knowing also that pusillanimity and idleness are most repugnant unto a reasonable creature and that (as the philosopher sayeth) even as an instrument of iron or of other metal waxeth soon rusty unless it be continually occupied. Even so shall the wit of a man, or woman, wax dull and unapt to do or understand anything perfectly, unless it be always occupied upon some manner of study, which things considered hath moved so small a portion as God hath lent me to prove what I could do.

And therefore have I (as for essay beginning, following the right notable saying of the proverb aforesaid) translated this little book out of French rhyme into English prose, joining the sentences together as well as the capacity of my simple wit and small learning could extend themselves. The which book is entitled, or named, The Mirror or Glass, of the Sinful Soul, wherein is contained how she (beholding and contemplating what she is) doth perceive how, of herself, and of her own strength, she can do nothing that good is, or prevaileth for her salvation—unless it be through the grace of God, whose mother, daughter, sister, and wife, by the scriptures she proveth herself to be.

Praying God Almighty, the maker and creator of all things, to guarantee unto Your Highness the same New Year's Day, a lucky and a prosperous year with prosperous issue and continuance of many years in good health and continual joy and all to His honour, praise, and glory."

From Ashridge, the last day of the year of our Lord God, 1544."

By Christmas of the same year, King Henry was thought near to death. Suffering with much pain, the king's court was closed for the holiday and only Katherine and Lady Mary were with him. He died just over a month later, on January 28, 1546. Prince Edward succeeded him under a Regency Council appointed by the late King Henry VIII, and Katherine moved to her manor house in Chelsea with a 7,000-pound income granted by Henry's will.

Having done her royal duty, Katherine wasted no time in marrying her true love, Thomas Seymour, the new king's uncle. The couple wed secretly in May of 1546 and did not inform King Edward or the Princesses Mary and Elizabeth until later in the year. The royal family was shocked and disappointed in Katherine for not offering their father a proper mourning period. Furthermore, the Seymours had placed themselves as potential usurpers of the young king's throne, a fact that could not have been missed by the clever Katherine. She married Thomas regardless of his political ambitions, and published *Lamentation of a Sinner* in 1547.

The next year, she invited Princess Elizabeth and young Lady Jane Grey to join her at Sudeley Castle, Gloucestershire, so they could continue their education under her tutelage. Though Elizabeth, then 14 years old, was still very close to her stepmother Katherine, the latter found her husband embracing the girl and had no choice but to send her from the estate.

Katherine became pregnant for the first time that same year but died soon after childbirth from the same sickness that had claimed Jane Seymour. Her daughter, Mary, seems to have died around the age of two. Thomas Seymour was executed the very next year for plotting against King Edward VI.

Chapter 19 – More Theories on Henry Tudor's Fertility

King Henry VIII accomplished a great deal during his 37-year reign, including the reformation of the English church, the creation of a viable English navy, and the renovation of Whitehall into a lavish palace. Still, it is Henry's six wives and his obsessive need for a male heir for which most people remember him. What we can probably never know is whether there was indeed some medical reason for all the problems Henry's wives had in delivering healthy children, male or female.

By no means was King Henry VIII infertile, since his first three wives conceived within the first year of marriage and his first two wives became pregnant multiple times. So, fertility aside, it does seem that potentially, there may have been something about Henry that made carrying a child to full term nearly impossible for his wives. From our modern perspective, the sheer volume of miscarriages, stillbirths, and infant or childhood deaths in the Tudor household seems nothing short of horrendous. Research on the subject abounds and yet we cannot know if an illness was at work or if the royal family simply had a very unfortunate infant mortality rate.

Tudor England was not an easy place for any child, royal or otherwise, with 25 percent of newborns dying within their first year of life and 50 percent dying before their tenth. If a total count is taken of all King Henry VIII's children, including miscarriages, there would have been eight to 10 potential royal children. Three of these survived into their teens, and two died as adults. Two long-lived children out of 10 is not an unusual statistic for those times, but it also isn't particularly good. Furthermore, though history tends to remember Henry as the king with no sons, one of those three surviving children was in fact a boy: Prince Edward. Henry also fathered Henry Fitzroy and potentially other illegitimate children as well.

Some medical historians theorize that there was a problem with the Tudor king's post-conception fertility, however, and that it might be linked to syphilis. Syphilis is a sexually-transmitted bacterial infection that can cause long-term symptoms like joint pain and dementia – both of which have been attributed to King Henry, especially in his later years. In pregnant women, active syphilis can cut the odds of delivering a healthy baby in half. This would explain the late-stage miscarriages suffered multiple times by Queen Catherine of Aragon and Queen Anne Boleyn, who would have contracted the illness from Henry himself.

Syphilis has been a popular theoretical diagnosis for King Henry VIII mostly because it not only could explain problems in the birthing chamber but also issues with the king's personality. Henry was not known by his contemporaries as a "Mad" king, but many historians do believe the king suffered a trauma in early adulthood that affected his brain and temper. Considering Henry an unpredictable tyrant, an idea that is not without some merit, these theories portray Henry as a calmer and more subdued king before his accident in January of 1536. Knocked unconscious by the thrust of his opponent's weapon, Henry suffered intensely and never participated in a jousting tournament again. Months later, he called for the trial and execution of a woman he'd moved political mountains for just three years earlier.

If the accident did permanently change the king's personality, which cannot be proven conclusively, it certainly did not damage his libido.

He took up with mistresses and remarried, producing a healthy baby in 1537 with Jane Seymour. After Jane's death there were no more reported pregnancies by any of the king's wives, though the king insisted he was virile and still able to perform sexually. But, in spite of assertions to the contrary that the ever-macho king made to his physician after not consummating his marriage to Anne of Cleves, modern doctors agree that it was unlikely that Henry could perform sexually at that point of his life due to his ill health.

Indeed, the fact that there were no reported pregnancies with Henry's last two wives seems to support later-onset infertility that had not been part of his physiology as a younger man. By his late thirties, Henry was obese, struggling with sores in both legs, and probably medically unable to consummate his marriages to Catherine Howard or Katherine Parr. If he did have sex with his last two wives, it was unlikely a common occurrence. After his annulment to Anne of Cleves, King Henry no longer spoke of the need for more sons. By that time, of course, he already had a male heir in the family.

Stress is another factor that may well have come into play in the Tudor household, since Henry's wives were immensely pressured to produce sons. Queen Catherine of Aragon became pregnant very soon after she was married to the 18-year-old king but delivered a stillborn daughter in her seventh month of pregnancy. Aware that her duty as queen was primarily to give birth to healthy children, including at least one son, Catherine felt immense guilt. She was a very devout Catholic and may have believed she'd done something to offend God and was being punished by having her child taken from her.

After one more stillbirth and the arrival of a boy in 1511 that died soon after delivery, her concern could only have grown more and more unbearable. She fasted to try to purify her body in the hopes of having a healthy child, which sadly could only have lowered her chances even more. Queen Anne Boleyn, in her time, was under at least as much stress as her predecessor to bring a son to term.

Princess Elizabeth was considered a joy in that Anne and Henry's match was fertile, but the succession of miscarriages following that first successful birth sickened the new queen and made her fear for her position by the king's side.

Both Catherine and Anne chided themselves horribly over their failure to breed boys for Henry. This level of stress, potentially combined with an illness on the part of the father, must have made for a very difficult time in carrying any child all the way to term. Inept medical procedures of the time only made the situation worse.

Whether syphilis, Kell-positive blood, unbearable stress, or a combination of factors were at work in the Tudor bedrooms will not likely ever be known. Nevertheless, the mystery has remained one of the main legacies of the great Tudor king.

Chapter 20 – The Illegitimate Children of Henry VIII

Henry Fitzroy may have been the only child born out of wedlock that Henry Tudor acknowledged, but given the king's well-known infidelities, Fitzroy is unlikely to have been the only son or daughter begat of an extramarital royal affair. Bessie Blount's second child, a daughter, has been attributed to Henry VIII, as well as at least six more from other mistresses. Each of these children were born healthy and lived into adulthood, which suggests that many others were stillborn or miscarried, as was so common at the time.

Clearly, King Henry had a soft spot for Elizabeth Blount, since he not only provided her with a very comfortable life after her departure from court, but also that her son was the only illegitimate child Henry ever claimed as his own. Of the many mistresses the king took up with throughout his time on the throne of England, only a small number have been remembered as such, and even these few were only known for the parts they played in the larger political intrigues of the day. A small number of Henry's lesser-known love affairs are remembered only by the progeny they produced, though he would never admit to any such thing. He may have been proud to note that several of those children attributed to him were very clever, successful, and rather artistic.

It is impossible to track the histories of every one of Henry VIII's children or alleged children, but for many descendants of these people that tenuous link to the Tudor family is precious. In addition to Henry Fitzroy, there were five other children with a somewhat credible claim to Henry Tudor's patronage. Their cases were made either by a public affair or a private expenditure on the part of the king.

Thomas Stukley

About one year after Henry Fitzroy was born, Jane Pollard gave birth to a son named Thomas Stukley. This was around the same time that Elizbeth Tailboys, Bessie Blount's second child, was born. Jane Pollard was the wife of Sir Hugh Stukley, and like the majority of Henry VIII's mistresses she was married very near the date she gave birth, which does give the boy's later claim of royal heredity more clout. It was neither Jane nor Hugh who spoke of young Thomas' secret connection with King Henry VIII, but Thomas himself when he grew older. A contemporary of Princesses Mary and Elizabeth and Prince Edward, he joyfully paraded himself as the son of the king with no repercussions from the royal family. It was said that the young man resembled his alleged father, a rumor Thomas reveled in.

The Stukleys lived in Devon, but when Thomas came of age he moved north to Exeter where he became a mentee of the Bishop of Exeter and King Henry's closest friend, Charles Brandon. Thomas became a talented soldier and fell in with Edward Seymour, a powerful member of King Edward VI's Regency Council after the death of King Henry. Seymour was unpopular and had designs on the throne, however, so after his arrest Thomas Stukley exiled himself in France. He also served in the French military for a time before returning to England with a letter of commendation from King Henry II of France.

Upon returning to England, Thomas Stukley tried to gain favor with Edward VI by revealing a supposed French plot to recapture Calais. Unfortunately, John Dudley was then the main regent behind the crown and he used Stukley's information to manipulate Henry II into an uneasy truce at Stukley's expense. Thomas was imprisoned in the Tower of London as the creator of the French plot.

Stukley was released but faced trouble with debts and was constantly involved on the fringes of potential treason plots. He fled England several more times during his life and once told Queen Elizabeth I, whom he referred to as "sister," that he believed he would be a prince one day. Ultimately, Stukley was killed at the Battle of Alcácer Quibir, part of an ongoing campaign to ally himself with Spain and Portugal against England. The year of his death was 1578.

Richard Edwardes

In 1525, Richard Edwardes was born to Agnes Blewitt Edwardes, wife of William Edwardes. Unlike Thomas Stukley, Richard and his family were very quiet about their connection to Henry VIII, if indeed it did exist. It is difficult to say how Agnes came into the presence or service of the king, because the Edwardes family was quite poor. Richard was the only member of the family who received his education at Oxford University's Corpus Christi College and went on to be named the head of the Chapel Royal at Windsor Palace. Richard's luxurious education is his descendants' main claim to support his link to a rich benefactor – namely, King Henry VIII.

Richard became a successful poet, playwright and musical composer. This was a special achievement, not only for a man from a poor family, but for any artist who lived during the golden age of England's theaters. It was under the reign of Queen Elizabeth I that England built its first theaters and embraced the non-musical performing arts. Richard Edwardes was a contemporary of William Shakespeare, having had at least one of his plays performed to an audience that included the queen herself. The title of his work was *Palamon and Arcite*, a play whose story was based on that of Chaucer's famous *The Knight's Tale*. Unfortunately, during the show, the stage collapsed and three people died.

Richard's play *The Excellent Comedie of two the Moste Faithfullest Freendes: Damon and Pithius* was also performed for Queen Elizabeth I during her infamous Christmas festivities of the 1564-1565 season. This time his work was shown successfully. *Damon and Pithius* is the only remaining play in print from Richard Edwardes, but several of his musical compositions remain in print to this day, as does a collection of his poems entitled *A Paradise of Dainty Devices*.

Richard died October 31, 1566.

Catherine and Henry Carey

One of Henry VIII's most controversial mistresses was the Lady Mary Boleyn, sister to his most famous queen, Anne Boleyn. It is not known how long Mary and Henry were lovers but the affair was a badly-kept secret at the Tudor court. Around the time the king married his mistress off to a rich husband, as was his way, the two were involved romantically which led to theories that Mary's first two children, born in 1524 and 1526, were fathered by Henry Tudor.

Catherine was the eldest child, Henry the younger. Both were named Carey after their mother's husband, William Carey. William was an important servant of the King and served as a Gentleman of the Privy Chamber. His family was wealthy and privileged even before Mary's sister became the king's new wife in 1533.

Both Catherine and Henry Carey were brought under the wardship of their aunt Anne Boleyn, which kept them very close to King Henry and ensured they were properly prepared for a future at court. Though the children no longer lived with their mother after the death of William Carey in 1528, they kept in contact until Mary Boleyn was banished from court for marrying William Stafford in 1534.

As Catherine grew up it was remarked that she resembled King Henry, and indeed the portraits believed to be her likeness show that classic shade of Tudor red hair. Catherine married Sir Francis Knollys, a politician who served under Henry VIII, Edward VI, and

Elizabeth I, in 1540. She served as a lady-in-waiting to Anne of Cleves and Catherine Howard before King Henry's death, and then went on to serve in the court of Elizabeth I. Queen Elizabeth never mentioned Catherine's rumored patronage but held her in the highest of positions among her ladies.

Catherine and Sir Francis had 14 children. Upon the lady's death in 1569, Catherine was buried at Westminster Abbey. The plaque there relates her to Henry VIII only through her aunt Anne Boleyn

As for Henry Carey, he received an excellent education at a monastic school, worked with private tutors, and went on to become a Member of Parliament representing Buckingham. Henry's cousin, Queen Elizabeth I, knighted him in 1558 and created him a Baron the next year. As the First Baron Hunsdon, Henry had an annual salary of 400 pounds and oversaw the production of lands in Kent and Hertfordshire as well as the manors of Hunsdon and Eastwick. One year after becoming Baron, Henry was made master of the queen's hunting hawks. The job earned him another 40 pounds per year.

Henry went on to become the Lieutenant General of the Queen's army during the northern rebellion of 1569-1570. His troops were victorious and his cousin very generous in her appreciation. In addition to military promotions, Elizabeth I made Henry the Keeper of Somerset House, the estate where she had lived as a deposed princess.

In his later years, Henry Carey patronized William Shakespeare's theater group and had an affair with the very young poet, Emilia Lanier. He lavished her with money, gifts and comfort for several years until she became pregnant. In full King Henry VIII-style, Carey married his mistress off to a cousin in 1592, gave her a large sum of money and stepped out of the picture. His illegitimate son, Henry Lanier, was born in 1593. Carey and his own wife, Anne Morgan, had 16 children.

In 1596, Henry Carey died a wealthy and successful man. He was buried at Westminster Abbey.

John Perrot

In 1528, John Perrot was born to Thomas Perrot and Mary Berkeley. Said to be the product of an affair between his mother and King Henry VIII, John actually did grow to strongly resemble the Tudor king. He had rich red hair and beard and was thought to have the confidence and temper of King Henry. Though Perrot's claim to royal patronage was largely posthumous thanks to his granddaughter's husband, his is a compelling story that comes with a rather telling portrait.

The Perrot family lived in Wales, but upon his coming of age John travelled to England to attempt to make the acquaintance of the man he hoped was his biological father. He had the good luck to become part of William Paulet's household in the 1540s which brought him into view of King Henry. Perrot's career was looking up until Henry's death in 1547, but his case was taken up by the Regency Council of Henry's heir, King Edward VI. Perrot was knighted on the very day of Edward's coronation.

John travelled to France with an English envoy intent on arranging the marriage of the realm's young king with the daughter of French King Henry II. The marriage never took place, but Henry II immediately liked John Perrot and offered him a position in his own court. Intent on making a name for himself in England, Perrot declined but accepted Henry II's offer to pay off his debts.

When Queen Mary I took the throne out from under her cousin Jane Grey, John Perrot found himself imprisoned on the charge of sheltering Protestant heretics at his property in Wales. Upon his release he kept his head down until Elizabeth I took power. Under the new queen, Perrot once again flourished. He was put in charge of the naval ships of South Wales, and given the new post of Lord President of Munster, Ireland.

The Presidency of Munster was arduous and required Perrot to battle against constant attacks by the Irish against the Queen's authority. During his time there, Perrot hung an estimated 800 people who fought against him. He hated the job and quit without the Queen's consent in 1573, but was forgiven upon meeting with the queen at her court. Afterward, John returned to Wales with the intention of living a quiet life. The plan was of no use, since Queen Elizabeth had ongoing need of her trusted naval servant. In the 1580s, Perrot was sent back to Ireland as Lord Deputy.

The appointment was as difficult as before. Perrot faced revolts by organized Irish clans and spent years forging diplomatic relations with the Irish. He was ruthless, creating enemies on all sides. When he returned to England and was elected Member of Parliament for Haverfordwest in 1589, enemies in Ireland accused him of treason against Elizabeth. They produced letters, apparently written by John Perrot to King Philip II of Spain, in which the author wished to ally with Spain against the English crown. On the basis of this evidence, in which John had referred to the queen as a "bastard" on several occasions, Perrot found himself imprisoned in the Tower of London. He died there in September of 1593.

Chapter 21 – The Legacy of Henry's Six Wives

It is interesting to note that King Henry VIII loved many women over the course of his life but was incredibly choosy about which of those might become his wife and queen. Though Elizabeth Blount was widowed by 1533 and could have provided Henry with the chance not only to take a new wife but to legitimize Henry Fitzroy, the king had no interest in such a plan. He was similarly uninterested in a formal union with Mary Boleyn, Mary Shelton, or any of his other mistresses.

Henry put a great deal of thought into his potential marital matches, right from his first wedding with Catherine of Aragon. He had a specific vision in mind each time he married, though that vision changed drastically from wife to wife. Henry sought out charismatic, talented, and popular girls of noble birth who he felt could bring something to the office of Queen of England. This forethought perhaps shows the emotional side of Henry VIII that was forever searching for the right woman with whom to make the kind of family his own mother and father had.

Above all, the six wives of King Henry VIII of England and Ireland were passionate and intelligent women. Regardless of their particular brand of education, the various Queens of England next to King Henry Tudor were clever, charming, and hungry for knowledge. They influenced the future Queen Mary I, Queen Elizabeth I and

King Edward VI, as well as helping reshape the way England perceived female rulers, leaders, thinkers and philosophers.

Catherine of Aragon was a beacon of hope for intellectual women of her age. She commissioned a book from Juan Luis Vives that was intended for young Mary Tudor: *The EDUCATION of a Christian WOMAN*. IT WAS RADICALLY FEMINIST FOR THE TIME, EXACTLY WHAT CATHERINE INTENDED FOR HER ONLY CHILD AND THE PRESUMED HEIR TO ENGLAND:

"From meetings and conversation with men, love affairs arise. In the midst of pleasures, banquets, dances, laughter, and self-indulgence, Venus and her son Cupid reign supreme...Poor young girl, if you emerge from these encounters a captive prey! How much better it would have been to remain at home or to have broken a leg of the body rather than of the mind!"

Catherine of Aragon is buried at Peterborough Cathedral.

The first queen's belief in female education would not die with her. Henry VIII's last wife, Katherine Parr, though Protestant, was just as dedicated to education for her stepdaughters as had been their true mothers. Elizabeth benefitted the most from Queen Katherine's teachings, not only becoming a religious expert but forming a love of literature and history that would last her entire life. The last of Henry VIII's queens was buried at the Sudeley Castle Chapel. Her remains were moved to the tomb of Lord Chandos in the 19th century after Sudeley lay in ruins.

Though very young and perhaps undereducated, Catherine Howard left behind a legacy of a different sort: that of the equality of the female spirit to that of the male. She was everything the king wanted and yet nothing he believed her to be. Though Henry and other men of his stature were expected to take multiple lovers, noble women were guarded carefully and punished for the same behavior. Little Catherine, left to her own devices as a largely ignored young girl, found joy in the company of boys and men and did nothing to rein in her natural desires. If nothing else, she proved to a conservative kingdom that women are every bit the same creatures as their male counterparts. Her death did not change that fact. The body of the executed girl was buried, unmarked, at the Chapel of St. Peter ad Vincula at the Tower of London, after her ladies-in-waiting wrapped her in a black cloak.

Anne of Cleves, Queen of England for only a few short months, is unfortunately best-known as Henry VIII's ugly wife. Looking more closely at her story, however, it seems possible that instead of having been unattractive, Anne of Cleves stands as proof of King Henry's unstoppable ego. In truth, Hans Holbein the Younger had only a fraction of the talent of future portrait painters, and none of his subjects were very well-portrayed despite his popularity as an artist. No one but the king and future biographers made any negative note of the girl's physical features, and yet it is largely this that Henry used as an excuse to rid himself of yet another wife. He may well have been impotent at that point in his life, having failed to impregnate the two wives who came after Anne of Cleves. Perhaps it was embarrassment and a general lack of interest that dissolved the marriage before it had even begun. Perhaps he truly found her unappealing.

For whatever reason, Anne lived a life of luxury as a reward for her quick-thinking and refusal to acknowledge the hurtful rumors about herself. She is buried in Westminster Abbey and memorialized there as a Queen of England.

As for Jane Seymour, Henry VIII himself recognized her most enduring legacy the moment she delivered little Prince Edward. It was the son the king had waited for through his entire reign, the reason he divorced Catherine of Aragon and lost his passion for the Catholic faith. Poor Jane didn't live long enough to see to the upbringing of her boy, but her good luck in producing a child of the male sex made her untouchable in the heart of Henry VIII, who cherished her most of all his wives. She softened her husband's heart to his daughters and helped convince him – though posthumously – to reinstate their births as legitimate. Her likeness was repeatedly used in court portraits with Henry after her death, even when other queens were on the throne. Jane was buried in St. George's Chapel in Windsor Castle in a grave King Henry had specially prepared for her. Following his death in 1547, Henry joined her there.

Finally, there was Anne Boleyn. The woman for whom Henry Tudor discarded his faithful and loving wife, detached himself from the power of the Pope of the Catholic Church, and declared England his own religious domain. Her legacy is unending, having produced one of the most beloved monarchs in English history: Elizabeth Tudor. Elizabeth's and Anne's blood are still connected to the British crown in a land that has long since welcomed and adopted its own special form of Protestantism. For her, Catholic idols were smashed, religious lands appropriated and countless lives lost – including, ultimately, her own. From Queen Anne Boleyn we have the modern monarchy, the Reformation, and the Anglican Church.

Her passionate affair with the King of England proved fruitful enough to keep England stable for well over half a century after the death of Henry's other two children. The furious king, now renowned for his unfaithful heart, may have killed his once-beloved mistress and buried her body in an unmarked grave at St. Peter ad Vincula, but Anne's title as Queen of England was revived under the rule of her daughter Elizabeth. During the reign of Queen Victoria, Anne's body was identified and marked on the marble floor of the church. Queen Victoria also had the spot at Tower Green paved where Anne Boleyn, Catherine Howard, and several others lost their lives on the executioner's block.

A memorial stands on the spot now, created by Brian Catling. Shaped like a pillow onto which the severed heads of the executed would rest, the memorial reads:

"Gentle visitor pause awhile: where you stand death cut away the light of many days: here jewelled names were broken from the vivid thread of life: may they rest in peace while we walk the generations around their strife and courage: under these restless skies."

Read more Captivating History Books

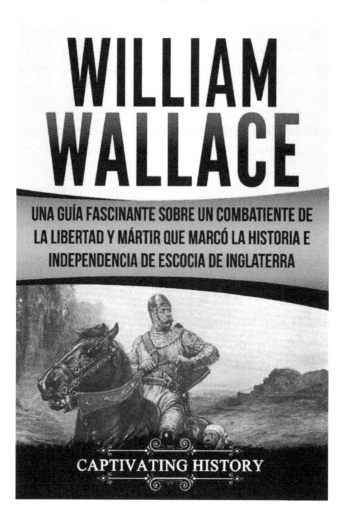

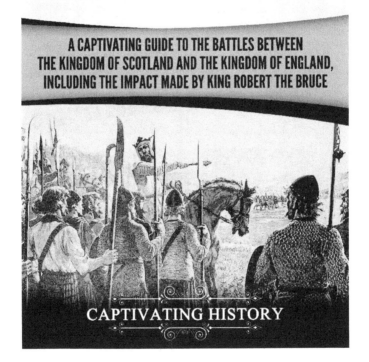

AZTEC

A Captivating Guide to Aztec History and the Triple Alliance of Tenochtitlan, Tetzcoco, and Tlacopan

CAPTIVATING HISTORY

INCAS

A CAPTIVATING GUIDE TO THE HISTORY OF THE INCA EMPIRE AND CIVILIZATION

CAPTIVATING HISTORY

References

Burnet, Gilbert (editor). Letter from Katharine of Aragon to her husband, King Henry VIII 16 September 1513. THE HISTORY OF THE REFORMATION OF THE CHURCH OF ENGLAND, Volume VI.

Calendar of State Papers Relating to English Affairs in the Archives of Venice, Volume 2, 614

Calendar of State Papers, Spain, Volume 4 Part 1: Henry VIII, 1529-1530, pp. 337-363, note 224, Letter from Eustace Chapuys to the Emperor, 6 December 1529.

Elizabeth I. "Letter to Katherine Parr, 1544." Transcribed by Anniina Jokinen. *Luminarium*. 10 Sept 2006. [accessed July 10, 2018]

Green, Mary Anne Everett (1846). Letters of royal and illustrious ladies of Great Britain, from the commencement of the twelfth century to the close of the reign of Queen Mary.

Hall, Edward. HALL'S CHRONICLE: CONTAINING THE HISTORY OF ENGLAND, DURING THE REIGN OF HENRY THE FOURTH, AND THE SUCCEEDING MONARCHS, TO THE END OF THE REIGN OF HENRY THE EIGHTH, IN WHICH ARE PARTICULARLY DESCRIBED THE MANNERS AND CUSTOMS OF THOSE PERIODS. CAREFULLY COLLATED WITH THE EDITIONS OF 1548 AND 1550, Printed for J. Johnson, 1809, p. 833.

Juan Luis Vives (1523). *The Education of a Christian Woman.*

Letters of Royal and Illustrious Ladies of Great Britain: From the Commencement of the Twelfth Century to the Close of the Reign of Queen Mary, Volume 1

Orchard, James. Letters of the Kings of England, Volume 1, 353. Halliwell-Phillipps.

Pascual de Gayangos (Editor) (1882). 'Spain: February 1533, 1-28', in CALENDAR OF STATE PAPERS, SPAIN, VOLUME 4 PART 2, 1531-1533, pp. 587-607. BRITISH HISTORY ONLINE http://www.british-history.ac.uk/cal-state-papers/spain/vol4/no2/pp587-607 [accessed 9 July 2018].

Rogers, E.F. (editor). Thomas More Selected Letters, 2-3, quoted in **Henry Virtuous Prince**, David Starkey, p143.

Wood, Mary Anne Everett (ed.) (1846). *Letters of royal and illustrious ladies of Great Britain, from the commencement of the twelfth century to the close of the reign of Queen Mary*, Volume II, Henry Colburn, p.193-197.

Free Bonus from Captivating History (Available for a Limited time)

Hi History Lovers!

Now you have a chance to join our exclusive history list so you can get your first history ebook for free as well as discounts and a potential to get more history books for free! Simply visit the link below to join.

Captivatinghistory.com/ebook

Also, make sure to follow us on:

Twitter: @Captivhistory

Facebook: Captivating History:@captivatinghistory

Made in the USA
Columbia, SC
13 March 2021